Blockchain: Trust Companies

Blockchain: Trust Companies

Every Company Is at Risk of Being
Disrupted by a Trusted Version of Itself

RICHIE ETWARU

Published by Dog Ear Publishing
4011 Vincennes Rd
Indianapolis, IN 46268
www.dogearpublishing.net

dog Kear
PUBLISHING

ISBN: 978-1-4575-5662-3

This book is printed on acid-free paper.

Printed in the United States of America

About the Author

Richie Etwaru brings breadth and depth in his experience as a C-level Fortune 500 Company executive, one of the first Chief Digital Officers in the world, a serial author, owner of international patents, founder of multiple ventures, an experienced keynote speaker, an angel investor, a member of advisory boards, the owner of restaurants, and a recognized thought leader in the area of digital, technology, and design.

Specific to this book, Richie is an adjunct professor of blockchain management at Syracuse University in New York. He has delivered over 100 blockchain keynotes across the world and has written some of the most read blockchain blogs as of this writing. His interviews on blockchain, advisory work with governments and venture funds, and TEDx talk titled "*Blockchain: Massively Simplified*" delivered in March 2017 has unlocked potential and identified opportunities for hundreds of organizations.

On a personal level, Etwaru is a thinker, a tinkerer, and a bit of an intellectual threat. He debates, deciphers and decides at the velocity of thought. This is a quality most of his friends, colleagues, and family prefer he slowed. He is married to his love Vashti, lives in Edgewater New Jersey, USA, and is a lover of spicy food.

For Aron Dutta

If I did not meet you, I would have never been inspired,
equipped, and focused enough to write this book.
I hope that everyone can meet someone like you
in his or her lives.

CONTENTS

About the Author vii

Foreword by R "Ray" Wang...1

Introduction 3

0. What to Expect 9

1. Cooperation and Control 11

    The Need for Control...16

    The Evolution of Human Organization 19

    Opportunity 1: Find Balance Between Cooperation
    And Control 23

2. Partnerships and Corporations 25

    Partnerships 26

    Corporations...30

    The Dutch East India Company 33

    Opportunity 2: Model The Modern Organization 38

3. Financial Control 39

    Double-Entry Bookkeeping.......................................41

    The General Ledger 43

Two Sets of Books..45

Cooking the Books 47

Sunbeam Fills Its Ledgers With Fraud.......................................48

Opportunity 3: Deliver on Consistent Financial Control...........51

4. The Flow of Wealth...53

The Widening Wealth Divide...56

Opportunity 4: Address The Trust Gap.....................................60

5. The Trust Gap 61

Enron: The Poster Child for Mistrust 64

So Many Ways to Commit Fraud..67

General Ledger Fraud 68

Identity Theft 69

Account Takeover 70

Collusion With Outsiders...71

Double Check Fraud 72

Opportunity 5: Restore Trust and Transparency.......................73

6. Big Data, Big Problems 75

The Catholic Church...75

Walmart...79

Opportunity 6: Deliver Data For Good 84

7. Spreadsheets Need to be Disrupted.....................................85

History is a Cycle of Disruptions 88

Opportunity 7: Get Out of Spreadsheet Hell 91

8. The New Corporate Models Aren't So New 93

Uber 96

Airbnb 100

The American Red Cross 104

Opportunity 8: Break Out Of Opaqueness 107

9. Enter the Blockchain Protocol 109

The Knowledge Gap 110

The Power Gap..112

The Distance Gap..114

The Growing Trust Gap...115

Blockchain Closes the Trust Gap..120

A Simplified Introduction to Blockchain 122

1. Authority Is Distributed Into The Network 123

2. Data Is Immutable...125

3. Security Is Managed By Keys and Signatures......................127

A Word About Bitcoin 131

10. From Abundant Trust to Consensus 137

Beyond Lowering Transaction Costs 139

La'Zooz...141

Music and Art..147

Blockchain and Real Estate 150

11. From Consensus to Autonomy 155

New Corporate Models: The Decentralized Autonomous
Organization..157

Smart Contracts...159

12. The Future: Trust Companies....................................167

Finance 169

Identity..170

Reputation...173

Inventory 174

Market...176

Agreement 178

Cooperate 180

The Future: Trust Companies 182

Blockchain: Trust Companies

Foreword
by R "Ray" Wang

The confluence of disruptive technologies on new business models have created massive opportunities for business transformation. In fact, on-going maturation in the digital world has resulted in more data, faster interactions, greater connectivity, and increased automation. Despite the benefits of digitization, the very basis of how companies are organized remains as cloogey and clunky as ever. Add the lack of trust and transparency, at a time of increasing technology acceleration, organizations and individuals face challenges with working with each other at digital scale.

Blockchain, also known as distributed ledger technologies, shows significant promise in addressing the trust and transparency required for a digital world. Opportunities exist to rethink cooperation and control, governance, financial control, flow of wealth, the trust gap, and transforming transparency of organizations. Consequently, society faces a unique opportunity with blockchain to transform how we engage with each other.

Almost every industry will be touched by blockchain. Whether regulated or not, organizations and individuals will gain the ability to drive down the cost of search, achieve consensus, enforce policies, exchange value, validate identity, orchestrate services, and reduce cost of intermediaries. Over time, the insights gained from the blockchain provide demand signals built on actions taken, not forecasts or hypotheses. These demand signals will not only deliver on mass personalization at scale, but also, provide insights into potential new offerings, and prevent potential conflicts such as adverse reactions, legal battles, and regulatory violations.

While the possibilities remain endless for blockchain to disrupt industries, the real value will come from the impacts to government and society. This notion of trust and transparency are paramount in the digital age. The meta data spurned off from engagement data guides policy makers improving trust and transparency. How? This data provides insights that identify and address inequalities, slowly restoring faith in institutions. Further, blockchain can reduce the friction involved in every interaction leading to trust companies, governments, and peoples.

Organizations must quickly take the first step toward disrupting themselves by piloting a use case and core business model around blockchain. The efficiencies achieved unlock the potential for massive innovation. Add the historical perspective, Richie has provided, leaders can apply lessons learned and advance their organizations into the future. Time is of the essence and blockchain will enable organizations to take back time, disrupt industries, and transform business models.

If you are faced with a binary choice to lead or be left out, this is one the books for you.

Introduction

It had been about three months since the day I sat in an airplane for the first time. Three months prior, I was leaving Guyana, full of dreams of a land where money grew in trees; the United States of America.

Of course in the United States there was no money to be found in trees, and no free rides. I was now sixteen after migrating to the United States of America three months prior, and getting accepted into college required that I provided documentation to show that I was both academically capable and of good health. Academically I had no hiccups. However, my Guyanese vaccination card that would serve as documentation of good health was missing handwritten evidence of enough vaccines, and the admissions officer at York College in Queens, New York who was responsible for evaluating my good health, suggested I get any two more vaccines if I were to enroll "without hiccups" for the upcoming semester. It seemed as if it did not matter that I had the important vaccines, I just needed two more, any arbitrary two.

"They are not that important, you just need to have two more," he said "any two will work".

My family had a few hundred dollars in savings since migrating three months back, and the fee would be a few hundred dollars to administer two arbitrary vaccines. I would have bankrupted my family to take any two additional vaccines of choice for reasons I still do not understand.

The good news was, I already had a summer job, and it would have taken me two months to save up the few hundred dollars needed to pay for the two arbitrary vaccines, the bad news was I would have missed starting college that upcoming semester. I could not afford at the time two arbitrary vaccines, and did not want to wait six months to start on the important business of learning how to learn in college, because of two unimportant arbitrary vaccines.

However, a pen was virtually free, I could afford one. It was easy to write the names of two vaccines on two blank lines on my vaccination card. I already had the basic required vaccines for sure, mumps, measles, rubella, polio, etc., and so I wrote into two rows onto my vaccination card the seasonal flu and chicken pox to simply have enough rows filled in. For sure I had temporarily tampered with my health record to get into college, on the argument from someone I did not trust who suggested that I simply needed two more arbitrary rows to avoid hiccups, which he could not explain.

I remembered this incident recently during my medical check-up when I turned forty. My doctor, a middle-aged progressive healthcare practitioner, commented on my main organs after the check-up, stating I had the heart of a twenty-seven-year-old, the lungs of a thirty-year-old, and he had never seen such strong health signals from a forty-year-old who rarely worked out, had a high-stress career, did not really eat well, and barely slept. I was surprised, I am pretty sure I am not that healthy.

I told him it was my good childhood vaccines. He chuckled, out of courtesy, but not because he understood my joke for one. Later that summer in 1992 about a week before my first day of college, I had saved up the few hundred dollars needed and went to a doctor and had the vaccines administered, I got the same ones I had hand written onto the vaccination card two months earlier, the seasonal flu and chicken pox. Who knows, maybe that's why I am somewhat healthy for my age, according to my vaccination card I have two seasonal flu and two chicken pox vaccines, administered two months away from each other in the summer of 1992.

Almost every piece of information about the analog world is about to be stored digitally. As a species we increasingly store inventory data, transaction data, identity data, reputation data, and corporate data along the corridors of history. With every new type of data stored, new areas of fraud erupt and new opportunities arise for entrepreneurs to build new frontiers of commerce and climb the wealth ladder, while those that don't participate in the building of new frontiers *become* that ladder.

The printing press, the steam engine, electricity, air travel, and the Internet all came with the opportunity for some to get wealthier by accelerating evolution, while others became martyrs of said evolution. For some large paradigms such as the Internet, the choice to take part in the acceleration of human evolution or stand by the sideline has a binary outcome. Just ask Blockbuster, Kodak, or Barnes & Noble.

I was not the first to be frustrated by the requirement to over vaccinate and temporarily *doctor* my vaccination card, no pun intended, and I won't be the last. Written paper records—or ledgers—are easy to doctor, but you can usually only doctor them one at a time, for yourself, or maybe a friend or a family member.

On the other hand, with a keyboard a single human being can tamper with large amounts of digital records—like the amount of money in an account, the ownership of an asset, or the reputation of a person. Manipulation of digital records can be done in large amounts instantly.

In 1992 I showed a US college admissions counselor a vaccination card from Guyana with handwritten entries, and he trusted the entries there but arbitrarily asked for two more. But if I walked into a college today and showed a college admissions counselor my mobile phone logged into a secure government website, with the records of my vaccination displayed on a screen, he/she would be unlikely to trust it. Digital data is not automatically trusted.

While we relish and simmer in an increasing sea of bubbling digital data about everything and almost anything, our hearts and our collective guts struggle with increased distrust for digital data. We know that most digital data can easily be tampered with in mass amounts, and as a result no person or organization can be fully trusted in a vacuum.

We increasingly start every company and every transaction with the automatic subliminal assumption that the counterparty cannot be trusted. We know that trust is the fundamental raw material of commerce, and we have learned that trust is delicate, poignant, hard to build, and easy to lose. We live in a trust gap.

Yet, the over 7 billion of us on Earth transact approximately $100 trillion of value between ourselves every year running on "trusted" processes or systems, and "trusted" data.

How do we do it? We *manufacture* the trust to transact, and we trust but verify. We trust but verify with centralized intermediaries, and as a failsafe we have contracts. As we transact with more parties (smart devices, and with each other in more ways over Apps like AirBnB and Uber), the trust gap increases, requiring more manufacture of trust.

We are living in an exponentially expanding *trust gap.*

Enter blockchain, a trust machine made from technology. Blockchain goes back to the beginning of time, and resets the playing field for all members of the human species.

It is an epic rethink of the ledger, the main structure of all data stored. It is an immutable and distributable ledger.

Blockchain presents the realistic opportunity that as a species we may soon get to a place where we can more fully trust data on a blockchain running asymmetric cryptography on immutable distributed ledgers abundantly because it will be very easy to identify data that was tampered with, like my temporarily tampered vaccination card needed to be admitted to college.

We are about to have the largest reset in commerce and adjustment to the pace of civilization driven by the emergence of abundant trust, and those who understand this reset first, stand to be able to repaint the world with their own brushes and colors.

I'm one messenger for the blockchain reset, or at least that's what I tell myself.

This is my book. I hope you enjoy it, and that it sparks new discussions, new ideas, and new actions.

0. What to Expect

This is a book, not a blog, a collection of blogs, or a re-arrangement of the thoughts of others. Expect a deep intro-spection on how commerce was initially created, what changes have transpired historically, and what has lead us to the state of untrusted and mistrusted commerce we are in today.

Each chapter sheds light on one crack that led to shattered state of trust we use to transact today. The end of the book discusses blockchain as a potential paradigm that could en-able us to go back and reinvent commerce in a way where it can be reinstated in its trusted form.

If you are interested in blockchain, this is not the only book you should read, but one of a handful. The book focuses on the problem that blockchain solves, the "so what" if I may of blockchain, more than the "what" of blockchain. After reading this book, my hope is that you the collective reader will join me in the crusade to bring this paradigm to life in a way where we can use it to reshape the human experience.

Not everyone will agree with my thoughts in this book, or at least I hope not! But I am hoping that everyone agrees that in some far off corner of the planet, some one person of the human species will read this book and decide "*I am going to dedicate my life's effort to bring this paradigm to life in a way that changes the world for the good.*"

If you are looking for snack-able shallow blips of intelligence or just a few pages of introspection, put this book down. This is an immersion.

1. Cooperation and Control

Ninety thousand years ago, at the dawn of human civilization, members of the emerging species known as *Homo sapiens* lived in a very dangerous world.

Predators, disease, and starvation were formidable enemies. Over time, people learned to survive by banding together, finding safety and support in numbers. Cooperation—the altruistic pooling together of skills and energy to achieve a common goal—proved to be essential when hunting, building shelters, and fighting enemies.

The history of human cooperation is particularly intriguing.

As compared with other primates, human beings are exceptionally cooperative, especially with people who aren't related to us. We live in large groups composed mostly of non-relatives, and we regularly help strangers, even when those interactions are unobserved and unlikely to be repeated.

But how exactly did we evolve to become cooperators? Aside from the obvious fact that cooperation produces positive results that benefit individuals within a group, there are numerous theories that attempt to explain exactly how and why humans became cooperative.

One theory comes from evolutionary psychology, and is often called the "big mistake" hypothesis. The basic idea is that human altruism—the principle or practice of concern for the welfare of others—evolved at a time when humans lived in small groups, comprised mostly of kin. In this setting, altruistic acts would either (a) benefit kin, which was a good thing, and so would evolve due to kin selection, or else (b) benefit the altruist by enhancing in some way his or her chances for reciprocity, which is especially critical in small groups in which reputational assessment among interacting members is constant. An individual who was predisposed to help fellow kin would likely have been compensated for his or her investment, either via indirect benefits to kin or via personal benefits arising from future interactions with the recipient.

The "big mistake" arose when a human behaved altruistically towards someone who was *not* a kin, and therefore the act would not benefit the altruistic person's family. Over time, such mistakes became commonplace, as people learned that there were benefits to helping non-kin.

While altruistic behavior such as kin selection and reciprocity can explain the behavior of small social groups common in many species, it's unable to explain the large complex societies of unrelated, anonymous individuals that we see in the human species. Thus emerged the idea of cultural group selection, which focuses on a later stage in human evolution characterized by larger social groups. The basic idea is that social groups with more altruists will, for various reasons, outcompete other groups in building value. The case for cultural group selection followed Darwin's conclusion regarding natural selection: If variation exists at the level of groups, and if this variation is heritable, and if it plays a role in the success or failure of competing groups, then selection will operate at the level of groups. As Darwin wrote in *The Descent of Man* in 1871, "Now, if some one man in a tribe, more sagacious than the others, invented a new snare or weapon, or other means of attack or defense, the plainest self-interest, without the assistance of much reasoning power, would prompt the other members to imitate him; and all would thus profit." This is the raw material for the motivation to compete.

Thus main transmission of such progress takes place not genetically but culturally. Modern humans are inclined to imitate others, and so if a group has altruists, others will often imitate them, and that will enhance the success of the group. As groups become larger in scale, those that foster social norms and institutions encouraging altruism will continue to thrive relative to others. Biological adaptations for altruism are not necessarily suggested, but the theory does allow for subsequent gene-culture coevolution in which individuals biologically adapt to life in a culture characterized by group competition, conformist social transmission, and group norms and punishment.

Another theory, proposed by Michael Tomasello and others, postulates that human cooperation isn't based on altruistic helping but rather a form of mutualistic collaboration. The theory of interdependence states that at some point humans created social systems in which collaborating with others was necessary for survival and procreation. This condition of interdependence gave rise to altruism, as individuals sought to help their collaborative partners on whom they relied for key activities such as foraging success. Interdependent collaboration also mirrors humans' unique traits of social organization and cognition, since it is not altruism but collaboration that creates the many coordination problems that arise as individuals attempt to put their heads together in acts of shared intentionality. This is the raw material for the motivation to corporate.

However it happened, as millennia passed humans very quickly learned to subsume their free will and cooperate on a scale unknown in the rest of the animal kingdom. Our Late Pleistocene ancestors—living roughly 126,000 to 12,000 years ago—inhabited the African savannah and other environments rich in large game animals, and where cooperation in acquiring and sharing food yielded substantial benefits at relatively low cost. The long growth period of human offspring, with children being dependent on their caregivers for many years, also encouraged the cooperation of non-kin in child rearing and provisioning. As a result, members of groups that created and sustained cooperative strategies for child rearing, food gathering, defending against enemies, sanctioning non-cooperators, and truthfully sharing important information had significant advantages over members of non-cooperative groups.

Soon, cooperative humans began to leave their marks on the earth. The oldest known evidence of constructed dwellings are the remains of six huts made of mud and branches, built by hunter-gatherers around 17,000 BCE at the Ohalo site near the edge of the Sea of Galilee. The Natufians built houses, also in the Levant, around 10,000 BCE. The Natufian communities may be the ancestors of the builders of the first Neolithic settlements of the region, which may have been the earliest in the world.

After the development of agriculture, remains of settlements such as villages become much more common. By about 7000 BCE, advances in agricultural production in the Middle East made it possible to support thousands of people, many of whom were not engaged in agriculture, in densely populated settlements. Two of the earliest of these settlements were at Catal Huyuk, in present-day southern Turkey, and Jericho, founded by the Natufians in what is today the Israeli-occupied West Bank. With populations of a few thousand people, Catal Huyuk and Jericho would be seen today as little more than large villages; but in the perspective of human cultural development they represented an emerging impulse toward mutual long-term cooperation.

Perhaps the crowning achievement of ancient cooperative effort was the construction of the Great Pyramid of Khufu at Giza, Egypt. While the earliest known Egyptian pyramid is the Pyramid of Djoser, found at Saqqara, northwest of Memphis, which was constructed between 2630 BCE and 2611 BCE, the Great Pyramid is the largest and most stupendous. Built as a tomb over a ten- to twenty-year period concluding around 2560 BCE, for more than 3,800 years the Great Pyramid was the tallest man-made structure in the world. It consists of an estimated 2.3 million limestone and granite blocks, which means that completing the building in twenty years would involve moving an average of more than twelve of the huge stones into place each hour, day and night, seven days a week. A modern construction management study has estimated that the total project required an average workforce of about fifteen thousand people, and a peak seasonal workforce of roughly forty thousand. Evidence suggests that around five thousand were permanent workers on salaries, with the balance working seasonal shifts while receiving subsistence wages. Some Egyptologists believe that the majority of workers may have been volunteers.

All of this speaks to a deep and strong impulse within the human spirit to come together, cooperate, pool talents and resources, and work together for a common goal.

If you can divorce from the fringe biases on the pros and cons of cooperation for human good, it becomes clear as day, that as a species we must cooperate in order to continue to thrive.

As you're no doubt thinking, to create these great monuments takes more than just an altruistic spirit of cooperation. After all, bee colonies are marvels of cooperation, and yet over many millennia bees have never managed to build the Great Pyramid. The logistical challenge of housing, feeding, disciplining, and paying the large army of ancient Egyptian workers required a high degree of administrative skill.

For big projects, cooperation needs to be married to leadership. Cooperation and control: in human society, the two have long gone hand in hand.

To provide our many efforts with the necessary structure of control, humans have done more than just cooperate. We tend to organize ourselves hierarchically, with a leader or group of leaders who had a vision of the future and authority over the cooperative efforts of the community.

Regardless of the form taken by the control element—there can be many—over the course of history people have shown a strong inclination to grant control to a leader, to entrust to a single person exceptional powers, and sometimes even allow themselves to be swayed by individuals who claim mystical leadership qualities that are beyond the understanding of ordinary people.

The first historical records of kings begins with the Sumerian King List, an ancient stone tablet originally recorded in the Sumerian language, listing kings of Sumer (ancient southern Iraq) from Sumerian and neighboring dynasties, their supposed reign lengths, and the locations of the kingship. The earliest listed Sumarian monarch whose historicity has been archaeologically verified is Enmebaragesi of Kish, who ruled ca. 2600 BCE. In Sumaria, as in many other cultures, kingship was seen as conferred by the gods, and therefore kings possessed proprietary sacred knowledge.

In Egypt, an enduring tradition of strong leadership took root at the same time. The Palermo Stone is one of seven surviving fragments of a stele known as the Royal Annals of the Old Kingdom of Ancient Egypt. The stele contained a list of the kings of Egypt from the First Dynasty (ca. 3150 to 2890 BCE) through to the early part of the Fifth Dynasty (ca. 2392 to 2283 BCE) and highlights of events during their reigns.

In the spiritual arena, humans have a long history of celebrating and subjugating themselves to shamans. A shaman is a person regarded as having access to, and influence in, the world of unseen spirits. Shamanism encompasses the premise that shamans are intermediaries or messengers between the human world and the spirit worlds. In a trance-like state during a ritual, the shaman enters supernatural realms or dimensions to obtain solutions to problems afflicting the community, with the understanding that he or she is in contact with forces beyond the reach of ordinary people.

In ancient Egypt, the pharaoh was a shaman, with a direct and literal connection to the gods. Today, while few cultures accept the idea that a human being is the manifestation of a divine power on earth, plenty of people look to religious leaders as having special insights unavailable to regular folk.

In the secular world, another word for "shaman" is "expert": the person who possesses knowledge not understood by ordinary people, and which is presumed to have special value to the community. This person might be a doctor, a politician, a business leader, or even an accountant at a big corporation with complex finances. What they all have in common is a proprietary knowledge that other people don't have and can't understand.

Nowhere in history has this been shown more clearly—and tragically—than in Nazi Germany, where in 1932 Adolph Hitler, after a decade of asserting that *he alone* knew how to organize and direct the German nation, got himself appointed chancellor by President Hindenburg. He continued to amass power, and the next year made himself absolute

Führer und Reichskanzler ("Leader and Reich Chancellor"). For the next twelve years his authority was unquestioned, until it all came crashing down in ruins.

Thus over the course of history we see the continuous tug of war between the urge to act cooperatively and democratically, and the opposing urge to instill in one person or group of people special knowledge and authority, compelling the group to organize around that person's authority.

Without question the need to cooperate as a species, and the requirement that said cooperation needed to be controlled and "organized" emerged.

The Evolution of Human Organization

The tension and balance between democratic cooperation and authoritarian organization has long been embodied in how human beings have organized themselves around a specific purpose.

Throughout human history, work—the creation of value— has often required organization. The capture of game and fish, the planting and sowing of fields, and the defense of the village required varying degrees of cooperation among members of the group. Communal activity of this type had important social implications. A leader was needed to organize and direct the group, set goals, and punish non-conformists. Because the basic social group was the family tribe, kin relationships—from the tribal chief down—formed the basis for the managerial hierarchy.

Over thousands of years, the development of hierarchies in partnership with increased cooperation can be seen to enable progressively more complex behaviors. From earliest recorded history until the fall of the Roman Empire, empires supplanted various smaller kingdoms and city-states that had developed during a process of consolidation of yet smaller associations of human beings. The degree of control exercised in these systems varied, but there was a clear progression toward larger more centrally controlled systems. This process was often driven by military force.

During the time of ancient empires, large-scale human systems executed relatively simple behaviors, and individuals performed relatively simple individual tasks that were repeated by many individuals over time to have a large-scale effect. The development of irrigation projects in such areas as Egypt and Mesopotamia led to the use of mass labor, to an organizational hierarchy for coordinating and directing these activities, and to an impersonal government control for ensuring proper distribution of the water.

The increasingly complex economy created a need for record keeping, so writing was born, of which the first examples come from the bookkeeping records of the storehouses in ancient Mesopotamia.

Centuries later, in the large estates, or *latifundia*, of the Roman Empire, the complex organization of work resulted in the creation of a hierarchy of supervisors. On the larger *latifundia* that developed from about the second century BCE, the owner was often absent because he had many scattered estates. Direction of the affairs of each estate was left in the hands of a bailiff, under whose direction slaves, numbering in the hundreds or even in the thousands, were divided into gangs charged with specific duties.

The organization of work, which in Europe reached a peak during the Roman Empire, declined as the empire waned. The political and social breakup and economic decay of the late empire reduced most of Western Europe to small-scale, self-sufficient economic units—kingdoms, duchies, and city-states.

Meanwhile, the oldest extant human organization on earth—the Roman Catholic Church—was taking form. Organized around the person of St. Peter, who was believed to be the spiritual heir to Jesus Christ and therefore possessing special proprietary knowledge and powers, the early Christian Church was loosely organized. In part to ensure a greater consistency in their teachings, by the end of the second century Christian communities had evolved a more structured hierarchy, with a central bishop having authority over the clergy in his city. Soon, bishops in politically important cities such as Antioch, Alexandria, and Rome exerted greater authority over bishops in nearby cities.

When Constantine became emperor of the Western Roman Empire in 312, he gave large grants of land and money to the growing Church and offered tax exemptions and other special legal status to Church property and personnel. Christians were freed from the fear of persecution and began to send out missionaries beyond the fringes of the Empire, taking the first steps in building the Church into a truly global organization.

By the sixth century, these gifts and later ones had combined to make the Church the largest landowner in the West.

Meanwhile, the financial infrastructure, in the form of banks, was slowly taking form. Banking depends upon two things: a form of currency or held value, and record keeping. Objects used for record keeping—"bulla" (inscribed pieces of clay used by the Sumerians) and tokens—have been recovered from within Near East excavations dating from 8000 BCE as records of the counting of agricultural produce. Commencing in the late fourth millennia, mnemonic symbols were used by members of temples and palaces to serve to record stocks of produce. A very early writing on clay tablet, the Code of Hammurabi, refers to the regulation of a banking activity of sorts within the Mesopotamian civilization of an era that dates to ca. 1700 BCE. (This is the same royal edict that promulgated "an eye for an eye, a tooth for a tooth.")

Over the centuries, innumerable bank-like organizations flourished from China to the Middle East to Europe. In 1157, the first modern-day bank was established in Venice as the Chamber of Loans, created to manage funding for the expansion of the empire under Doge Vitale II Michiel. Changes in the enterprises of the Chamber led to the development of the organization into The Bank of Venice. The bank was the first national bank to have been established within the boundaries of Europe, and operations continued until the bank was shuttered during the French invasion of 1797.

Beginning in the fifth century, European trade and town life revived in the form of the new feudal society. The growth of interregional commerce stimulated demand for human organizations capable of extracting and holding value from increasingly large-scale trading systems.

During the late Middle Ages and Renaissance, industry pro-liferated, spurred by five factors: (1) the geographical growth of markets, first into Asia and then the New World, (2) the societal growth of markets fueled by the moneyed bour-geoisie, (3) the amassing of wealth, derived partly from the influx of precious metals from the New World but also from developments in commerce, banking, and the very concept of money, (4) the development of new technologies, and (5) the introduction of new products produced by specialized workshops. These helped increase the scale of manufactur-ing industries throughout Europe, which in turn prompted changes in the organization of work.

Against this backdrop, it was inevitable that humans would form increasingly complex organizations—corporations—for the creation, storage, and distribution of value.

Opportunity 1: Find Balance Between Cooperation And Control

As we cooperated, and organize in hierarchies where those with centralize power lead the coordination of value creation, capture and transfer – the need for "rules" governing how we organize emerged. Coopera-tion and control became increasingly dependent on each other as the size of an organization increased, can you keep this delicate balance while scaling?

2. Partnerships and Corporations

The idea of joint ownership of an asset is very ancient. No doubt our primitive ancestors, when figuring out how to allocate ownership rights and responsibilities among individuals who together occupied a cave, were able to construct a framework or set of rules that allowed for peaceful co-ownership of the dwelling. If one member left or died, then that would open up space for a new co-owner to move in. When value was created—a game animal killed or a basket of nuts collected—there was a mechanism for sharing that value equitably.

Therefore it wouldn't be such a large step to codify the relationship and even agree that the ongoing collective relationship— for example let us say we call it Cave Company—had an existence that transcended the participation of any one individual member. Therefore a common action taken by the individual members constituted not just an action taken by a bunch of people who happened to agree on something, but an action taken by Cave Company as a legal entity unto itself.

As we saw in the previous chapter with banks, the formation of an entity like our fictional Cave Company becomes necessary when you've got three things: an agreed-upon set of personal relationships among the members, a method of keeping records, and ongoing cooperative value creation. You need to track the value being created—the number of fish caught or nuts collected—and the disbursement of these assets, either to the members of the group or for sale or barter to outsiders. This means there are both *inter-organizational* rules and consensus and *intra-organizational* rules and consensus. The "inter" is the organizational operating model, while the "intra" is comprised of the smart contracts that enable frictionless commerce.

Partnerships

Most likely, the entity we are imagining known as Cave Company was a partnership.

A partnership is a single business where two or more people share ownership. Each partner contributes to all aspects of the business, including money, property, labor or skill. In return, each partner shares in the profits and losses of the business.

Generally, partnerships are defined by a written partnership agreement. The agreement documents how the partners will make investments, divide profits, resolve disputes, change ownership (bring in new partners or buy out current partners), and dissolve the partnership.

Since partnerships aren't recognized as legally distinct "people," they don't pay income taxes. Nowadays, in the United States a partnership must file an "annual information return" to report the income, deductions, gains, and losses from the business's operations, but the business itself does not pay income tax. Instead, the business "passes through" any profits or losses to its partners, who are required to include their respective share of the partnership's income or loss on their personal tax returns.

While partnerships are generally an inexpensive and easily formed business structure, there are risks. Like sole proprietorships, partnerships retain full, shared liability among the owners. Partners are not only liable for their own actions but also for the business debts and decisions made by other partners. In addition, the personal assets of all partners can be used to satisfy the partnership's debt. In the case of Cave Company, if one caveman sells a load of rotten fish to a neighboring tribe, each and every member of Cave Company can be held personally liable for the expected lawsuit.

Partnerships have a long history, being already in use in the Middle Ages in Europe and the Middle East. Traders would do business through common law constructs, including partnerships. Whenever people acted together with a view to profit, the law deemed that a partnership arose. Early guilds and livery companies were also often involved in the regulation of competition between traders.

In Europe, partnerships contributed to the Commercial Revolution, which started in the thirteenth century. Some guilds gradually transformed into family partnerships (*fraterna compagnia*), in which profits, common administration of real estate, and other property were shared by shareholders. These arose in the thirteenth century, notably in Venice, where mutual agreements to collaborate in business ventures facilitated greater trading volume. Likely these were profit-motivating deals in which collusion offered monetary benefits; in the unregulated environment of medieval Europe, collaboration might have given merchants access to more markets. It was, undoubtedly, a more chaotic "Wild West" environment than we are used to today. In absence of rules and regulations, trust was the key to reducing risk.

We can see early instantiations of trust still alive today in the global network of *hawala* money transfer agents. The hawala system—the word is Arabic for either "transfer" or "trust"—is a popular and informal value transfer system that originated in the eighth century between Arabic and Muslim traders alongside the Silk Road and beyond as a protection against theft. Based on the performance and honor of a huge network of money brokers, primarily located in the Middle East, North Africa, the Indian subcontinent, and Southeast Asia, the hawala system operates outside of, or parallel to, traditional banking, financial channels, and remittance systems.

The system is simple and decentralized. Let's say a customer approaches a hawala broker in Cairo and gives him fifty dollars that is to be transferred to a family member in Mumbai. A password is created that will permit the money to be paid out on the other end. The hawala broker in Cairo contacts another hawala broker in Mumbai, and informs Mumbai about the agreed amount, password, and other details.

No funds are exchanged or transferred. The hawala broker in Cairo *keeps the customer's money* and adds it to his capital reserves.

In Mumbai, the intended recipient, who has been informed by the customer in Cairo about the password, goes to the Mumbai broker and tells him the agreed password. The Mumbai broker goes into *his own money supply* and gives the recipient fifty dollars minus a commission. The Cairo broker now owes the Mumbai broker fifty dollars, and they promise to settle the debt at a later date.

If there are continuous exchanges between the brokers in Cairo and Mumbai, over time—a week or a month—it's possible that each side will record a net change of zero in their operating capital, as money is paid out and deposited.

Clearly, for such a decentralized system to work requires absolute trust between brokers.

How large is the system? No one knows!

As the International Monetary Fund wrote in 2003, "Estimating the size of hawala and other similar transactions cannot be undertaken with any reliability."

The U4 Anti-Corruption Resource Centre wrote, "The extent of hawala systems has been little explored in the literature and cannot be quantified reliably and accurately given the informal nature of the transactions. It is impossible to provide a precise figure, but it is likely that it ranges to billions of US dollars. Some countries make estimates based on their expatriate community and balance of payment data. In Pakistan, officials estimate that more than five to seven billion US dollars enters into the country every year through hawala channels.... In the case of India, Interpol estimates the size of hawala at possibly 40% of the country's gross domestic product. It is estimated that globally between USD 100 billion and USD 300 billion flow through informal remittance systems every year."

Who owns hawala? Nobody. Who controls hawala? Nobody. This is not to say there aren't big hawala networks. According to ArabCin.net, the largest hawala dealer or money transfer business is Dahabshiil, employing over two thousand people in more than 144 different countries. But in general, it's decentralized. Only the integrity of its thousands of peer-to-peer relationships keep it running. Hawala is a rare example of a cooperative human effort that has no need of a leader or control figure.

Corporations

Partnerships are fine for some purposes, but they're limited in how much capital they can raise, and the liability aspects can be enough to scare away big investors. From antiquity, people have been trying to figure out the best way to structure an organization that is flexible, offers protection from liability, has clear ownership demarcations, and provides a vehicle for raising money for big projects, like sending a merchant ship on a two-year voyage from Venice to India.

Entities that carried on business and were the subjects of legal rights have been found in ancient India and in Rome. Cities were the first entities the Romans treated as corporations. Over time, the concept was extended to certain community organizations called *collegia*, which included religious societies, artisan associations, and social clubs formed to provide funerals for members. By the time of Justinian (reigned 527–565 CE), Roman law recognized a range of corporate entities that included the state itself (the *populus Romanus*), municipalities, and such private associations as guilds of craftsmen or traders and political groups. The word "corporation" derives from "*corpus*," the Latin word for body, or a "body of people." Such legally recognized bodies commonly had the right to own property and make contracts, to sue and be sued, to receive gifts and legacies, and, in general, to perform legal acts through representatives. The emperor also granted to private associations designated various privileges and liberties.

Eventually, the definition of a "corporation" usually referred to joint-stock limited liability corporations that satisfied three conditions:

1. Legal "personhood." Corporations are treated as artificial people, with a capacity for legal rights and obligations similar to those of natural persons.

2. Equity financing. Ownership is securitized as stock that may be held by multiple investors and traded in secondary markets.

3. Limited liability. The liabilities of the corporation are not shared by its owners, who can lose nothing more than the capital they have already committed to the corporation.

In medieval Europe, churches became incorporated, as did local governments. The goal was that the incorporation would survive longer than the lives of any particular members, existing in perpetuity. For example, the City of London Corporation first recorded Royal Charter dates from around 1067, when William the Conqueror granted the citizens of

London a charter confirming the rights and privileges that they had enjoyed since the time of Edward the Confessor. Numerous subsequent Royal Charters over the centuries confirmed and extended the citizens' rights.

The sixteenth century gave rise to mercantilism, the economic theory and practice common in Europe until the eighteenth century that promoted governmental regulation of a nation's economy for the purpose of augmenting state power and wealth at the expense of rival nations. Precious metals, such as gold and silver, were deemed indispensable to a nation's wealth, and if necessary should by obtained by trade. Imports were to be restricted to necessary raw materials, which were then value-added to become finished goods for both domestic consumption and export. Colonial possessions, where manufacturing was forbidden, should serve as markets for exports and as suppliers of raw materials to the mother country. Of course, the impact of the discovery of the Americas was enormous, and new markets and new mines propelled foreign trade to previously inconceivable volumes. All of this was happening as technological advances in shipping and the growth of urban centers led to a rapid increase in international trade.

As the age of mercantilism progressed, merchants seeking to band together to undertake ventures requiring more capital than was available to any one merchant or family formed charter companies. A chartered company is an association formed by investors or shareholders for the purpose of trade, exploration, and colonization. From the sixteenth century onwards, groups of European investors formed companies to underwrite and profit from the exploration of Africa, India, Asia, the Caribbean and North America, usually under the patronage of one state, which issued the company's charter. The charter usually conferred a trading monopoly upon the company in a specific geographic area or for a specific type of trade item.

The earliest English chartered companies were the Merchant Adventurers and the Merchant Staplers. The former, chartered in 1407, was a company of English merchants engaged in the export of finished cloth from the burgeoning English woolen industry to the Netherlands, and later northwest Germany. The Merchant Staplers was incorporated by Royal Charter in 1319 for dealing in wool, skins, lead, and tin, and which controlled the export of wool to the continent during the late medieval period. Amazingly, the company—the oldest mercantile corporation in England—still exists. Based in Yorkshire, it makes charitable contributions through bursaries and awards to charities involved in the wool business, and to educational travel.

The Dutch East India Company

No discussion of the development of corporations would be complete without a review of one of the biggest and most powerful organizations ever to straddle the globe.

The story begins not in the Netherlands but in England, on December 31, 1600, when Queen Elizabeth I granted a royal charter to The Company of Merchants of London Trading into the East Indies. Established with 125 shareholders and £72,000 of capital, Sir Thomas Smythe was appointed as the company's first governor. Queen Elizabeth I also limited the liability of the investors as well as her liabilities in granting a

Royal Charter. This made The East India Company—as it was soon known—the world's first limited liability corporation.

It's a very important to note that a limited liability corporation *cannot exist* without the validation and support of a *strong central government.* Why? Because the members of the corporation have declared that their personal liability is limited only to the money they've put in, and no more. This assertion needs to be backed up by *power.*

Imagine if our fictitious Cave Company LLC—a limited liability corporation—sells a load of rotten fish to a customer, the Mountain Folk. People get sick and the Mountain Folk sue the Cave Company. The stockholders of Cave Company LLC reply, "You can sue us, but since we're an LLC, we assert that none of us are personally liable for more than we have invested."

The Mountain Folk say, "So what? We're going to attack you and destroy your cave and take everything that belongs to you. We don't care about your silly limited liability whatever-it-is."

But then the ruler of the Cave Folk, King Tough Guy, says, "I personally approved Cave Company's charter. I'm the law around here, and I have a big powerful army. If you mess with Cave Company, you mess with me."

The Mountain Folk reply, "Whoa! Cool off, King Tough Guy. Okay, we'll forget about physically attacking Cave Company. We'll resolve this in court."

In Elizabethan England, for a period of fifteen years the charter gave the newly formed East India Company a monopoly on trade with all countries east of the Cape of Good Hope and west of the Straits of Magellan—essentially all of the land masses touched by the Indian and Pacific Oceans.

Having pooled the resources of the 125 shareholders, in 1601 the first expedition of five vessels left Woolwich for the Spice Islands or East Indies—the Indonesian archipelago of the Moluccas (or Maluku Islands). The group was led by James Lancaster, who was armed with six letters of introduction from the queen, each with a blank space for the name of the local monarch. Lancaster intended to trade iron, lead, and British broad cloth for spice.

In 1602, across the North Sea in the Netherlands, the Dutch government took note of this threat and responded by sponsoring the creation of a single United East Indies Company and granting it a monopoly over the Asian trade. With a capital of 6,440,200 guilders, the charter of the new company—in Dutch named Vereenigde Oost-Indische Compagnie, or VOC—empowered it to maintain armies, build forts, and conclude treaties with Asian rulers. It provided for a venture that would continue for twenty-one years, with a financial accounting only at the end of each decade.

As joint stock companies, both the British East India Company and the VOC were private mercantilist tools with a guarantied trade monopoly in exchange of rights paid to their respective governments.

Of course, it's far easier for a monarch in Europe to grant a monopoly than to enforce it on the other side of the globe, so both British East India and VOC ships were heavily armed and empowered as governmental proxies to hire troops, establish colonies, take military action, and mete out justice in whatever manner was most expeditious to seizing markets and maximizing profits. This included arrest, imprisonment, and execution of any indigenous person who didn't cooperate.

In 1620, competition with the British East India Company led to diplomatic agreements in Europe that ushered in a period of co-operation between the Dutch and the English over the spice trade. Eventually the English quietly withdrew from most of their Indonesian activities and focused on other Asian interests.

By 1669, the VOC was the richest private company the world had ever seen, with over 150 merchant ships, forty warships, fifty thousand employees, a private army of ten thousand soldiers, and a dividend payment of forty percent on the original investment.

The VOC pioneered the novel idea that the liability of not just the *participanten* (non-managing members) but also of the *bewindhebbers* (managing directors) was limited to the paid-in capital; usually, bewindhebbers had unlimited liability. The VOC therefore was a limited liability company. It was the first company to give any citizen the opportunity to buy a share of the company to finance its activities. The period 1630-1650 saw the first modern securities market, and increased trading on the derivatives market was the main event. A liquid market was the result, and because of the interaction between traders, price discovery—a method of determining the price for specific merchandise through basic supply and demand factors related to the market—was possible.

Where there are profits and power, conflict among members soon follows. On January 24, 1609, Isaac Le Maire, a major shareholder of the VOC, filed a petition against the VOC. He formally charged that the VOC's board of directors (the *Heeren XVII*, or Lords Seventeen) sought to "retain another's money for longer or use it ways other than the latter wishes," and demanded the liquidation of the VOC. LeMaire was no angel; in 1605 he had been ousted by other governors on charges of embezzlement. Having retained stock in the company following this incident, Le Maire would become the author of what is celebrated as the first recorded expression of shareholder advocacy at a publicly traded company.

In 1622, VOC investors staged history's first recorded shareholder revolt when they charged that the company's account books had been "smeared with bacon" so that they might be "eaten by dogs." The investors demanded a "*reeckeninge,*" a proper financial audit. The 1622 campaign by the shareholders of the VOC is an early example of corporate management being accused of secrecy and self-enrichment—and it would hardly be the last.

By the eighteenth century the VOC had evolved from a commercial trading enterprise to a loose territorial organization focused on the agricultural produce of the Indonesian archipelago. Toward the end of the century the company became corrupt and seriously in debt. The company failed to raise additional capital when necessary, to limit borrowing, or to fund capital expenditures through cutting its dividend. The French Revolution of 1789 exerted a particularly negative effect on the company. In 1795, the revolution's forces entered the Netherlands, occupying the country and bringing about the birth of the Republic of Batavia. The Dutch government eventually revoked the company's charter, and in 1799 took over its debts and possessions.

Opportunity 2: Model The Modern Organization

Templates of how we organize and govern such as partnerships, corporations, or nonprofits have not be updated in centuries, we still use many of the ancient rules and vernacular today, patching expanding gaps of trust and accounting all stemming from increasing modernized complexity. What are the organizational structures of your entities that cooperate, and are they optimized for the speed and complexities of modern commerce, while maintaining trust and transparency at high levels?

3. Financial Control

Since the days of Cave Company, people have found it necessary to maintain records of contracts and transactions. Such records serve two purposes:

1. To act as a way to resolve disputes. If Cato complains that Titus cheated him on an expected delivery of ten bushels of rice, an independent record exists that confirms Titus was to deliver ten bushels.

2. To act as system of measurement. That is, if you have fifty bushels of rice and you barter away ten, you should have forty remaining.

Today, to record monetary transactions we use journals and ledgers. In a large organization, detail-level information for individual transactions is stored in one of several possible journals, while the information in the journals is then summarized and transferred (or posted) to a ledger.

Perhaps the oldest known journals are a collection of Egyptian papyri dating from 2560 BCE. As *Smithsonian Magazine* reported, in 2013 CE—over 4,500 years after the papyri were created—a French archeologist named Pierre Tallet made a stunning discovery: in a set of thirty caves honeycombed into limestone hills in a remote part of the Egyptian desert, a few miles inland from the Red Sea, far from any city, he came upon dozens of very ancient papyrus rolls.

The papyri were written by men who participated in the building of the Great Pyramid, the first and largest of the three colossal pyramids at Giza just outside modern Cairo. Among the papyri was the journal of a previously unknown Egyptian official named Merer, who led a crew of two hundred men who traveled from one end of Egypt to the other, picking up and delivering various goods. Merer, who accounted for his time in half-day increments, mentions stopping at Tura, a town along the Nile famous for its limestone quarry, filling his boat with stone, and taking it up the Nile River to Giza. He then reported to "the noble Ankh-haf," who was known to be overseeing some of the construction of the Great Pyramid.

Bookkeepers as we know them today most likely emerged while society was still in the barter and trade system (pre-2000 BCE) rather than a cash and commerce economy. Ledgers from these times read like narratives with dates and descriptions of trades made or terms for services rendered.

For example, an ancient Egyptian journal might have included the following barter records:

On the 12th day of the second month of Akhet: In exchange for one ox delivered to him, Osman the farmer promised fifty bushels of wheat when the harvest is completed in the fall.

On the 20th day of first month of Peret: Eraz the coppersmith agreed to make one cooking pot in exchange for one month of eggs from one hen, to be delivered as they are laid once the pot is finished.

Such transactions were kept in individual journals, either in the local temple or town hall; and if a dispute arose, they provided proof when matters were brought before magistrates. Although cumbersome, this system of detailing every agreement was necessary because long periods of time could pass before transactions were completed.

Double-Entry Bookkeeping

With the advent of currency over bartering, an important innovation was the introduction of double-entry bookkeeping and modern accounting. In the double-entry accounting system, at least two accounting entries are required to record each financial transaction. Recording of a debit amount to one or more accounts and an equal credit amount to one or more accounts results in total debits being equal to total credits for all accounts in the general ledger. For example, if $100 is received for the sale of one widget (credit), then $100 must be entered as a debit to reflect the lost value of the widget that is now no longer in inventory. If the accounting entries are recorded without error, the aggregate balance of all accounts having debit balances will be equal to the aggregate balance of all accounts having credit balances.

As another example, if investors put up $1 million for a company, then that $1 million must be recorded both as an asset—because the company owns it—and as a liability, because the investors, as owners, can lay claim to it.

The oldest discovered record of a complete double-entry system is the *Messari* ("Treasurer's") accounts of the Republic of Genoa in 1340. The *Messari* accounts contain debits and credits journalized in a bilateral form, and include balances carried forward from the preceding year. It was not a commonly used system; the credit for codifying double-entry bookkeeping goes to Luca Pacioli, a Venetian monk, magician, and lover of numbers. He became aware of this innovative bookkeeping method in Venice and was intrigued by it. In 1494, he wrote a massive math encyclopedia and included an instructional section on double-entry bookkeeping. By the end of the century, the bankers and merchants of Florence, Genoa, Venice and Lübeck were using this system widely.

Before double entry, merchants just kept diaries and counted their money at the end of the day. Double entry accounting precisely documented the inflow and outflow of trade, contributing to the close scrutiny given to the balance of trade. And, as we will see later in this book, the accountant or person who kept the ledgers was a key member of any organization, with tremendous power to either keep clean books or contribute to fraud.

One of the earliest cautionary tales about the value of good accounting comes from the court of King Louis XIV of France. His famed finance minister Jean-Baptiste Colbert commissioned miniature golden calligraphy account books for the Sun King to carry in his coat pockets. Starting in 1661, twice a year Colbert would deliver to the king updated accounts of his expenditures, his revenues, and his assets. This was an early exercise in modern governmental accountability: a king who carried his accounts so that, at all moments, he might have some reckoning of his wealth.

All went well until 1683, when Colbert died. Louis—consistently pushing spending limits to satisfy his predilection for costly wars and sumptuous palaces like Versailles—abandoned the account books. He began breaking up the central administration of his kingdom, making it impossible to unify the accounts of each ministry into one clear, central ledger, as Colbert had done, and for any minister to understand the king's financial management. The finances of the state fell into disarray, and on his deathbed in 1715, Louis admitted that he had bankrupted France with his spending.

The General Ledger

The core component of double entry bookkeeping was, and still is, the ledger.

Over the centuries, the ledger has become the principal book or computer file for recording and totaling economic transactions measured not in pigs or eggs but in terms of a monetary unit, with debits and credits in separate columns and a beginning monetary balance and ending monetary balance for each account. It serves as the permanent summary of all amounts entered in supporting journals, which list individual transactions by date. Every transaction flows from a journal to one or more ledgers. A company's financial statements are generated from summary totals in the ledgers.

The general ledger is the backbone of any accounting system holding financial and non-financial data for an organization. The collection of all accounts is known as the general ledger. Each account is known as a ledger account.

Each account in the general ledger consists of one or more pages. The general ledger is where *posting* to the accounts occurs. Posting is the process of recording in the pages of the general ledger transaction amounts as credits (right side), and amounts as debits (left side). Additional columns to the right hold a running activity total (similar to a checkbook).

The double-entry bookkeeping system helps ensure that the general ledger is always in balance, thus maintaining the accounting equation:

Assets = Liabilities + (Shareholders' or Owners' equity).

Therefore if a company has $50 million in assets, it must have $50 million in total liabilities. If the *actual* liabilities—such as taxes owed, lease payments owed, vendor payments owed—exceed assets, then the equation must be balanced by making the shareholders' or owners' equity a *negative number.*

Does this mean the shareholders need to open their checkbooks? Not really. Negative shareholder equity is often the result of the accounting methods used to reconcile accumulated losses from prior years. These losses are often viewed as liabilities carried forward until future cancellation. Oftentimes, the losses exist on paper only, which makes it possible for a company to maintain operations despite the continued posting of substantial losses.

Other situations that can contribute to negative shareholder equity are severe depreciation in currency positions, leveraged buyouts (or borrowing), and substantial adjustments to intangible property (patents, copyrights, or goodwill).

Just as accounting methods can produce negative shareholder equity that may be less alarming than you'd think, the opposite can also be done: a set of books can be massaged to make it look like shareholder equity is a much bigger positive number than it really is. You do this by either inflating assets or discounting liabilities, or both.

In the next chapter, we'll see just how commonly ledgers have been manipulated to meet a preconceived goal.

Two Sets of Books

The concept of "two sets of books" refers to having not one but two ledgers. By using accounting loopholes or interpretations of tax law, one ledger can reflect one financial "reality" while the other ledger can assert a different financial "reality."

The *legitimate* practice of keeping two sets of books is so publicly traded companies can prepare financial statements designed to please different stakeholders: the US Securities and Exchange Commission, the company's investors, and sometimes the Internal Revenue Service.

Many publicly traded companies use this practice and it is legal. When preparing financial statements for investors, they abide by the rules set by the Federal Accounting Standards Board, or the FASB, and when preparing tax returns they abide by the Internal Revenue Code. The goal here is to *maximize* income for the investors' financial statements, so when investors see them they will be eager to buy stock.

On the other hand, the company wants to *minimize* income on the tax returns, so they can pay less in taxes.

You can do this because, in our modern era of credit, it's not always clear when a financial transaction takes place.

For a simple example, let's say Cave Company sells one hundred chickens to Mountain Folk. The sales agreement is signed and dated August 20, which is the third fiscal quarter (Q3). The chickens are actually delivered on December 10, which is Q4. The Mountain Folk pay for the chickens on January 15, which is Q1 of the following tax year.

If you're the Cave Company accountant, on what date do you post the income from the sale?

You could post it in Q3, because you have a contract that has legal value. You could post it in Q4, which is when Mountain Folk took control of the chickens. Or you could post it in January, when the money actually entered your bank account. Of course, it is a bit more complex than this, but you get the point.

If the boss of Cave Company said, "To please our investors, we need more sales posted in Q4," the accountant might oblige by posting the sale as having occurred in December.

If the boss of Cave Company said, "We need to lower our taxable income this year," the accountant might oblige by posting the sale in January of the following year.

It's the same sale, but how it's recorded can change the short-term appearance of the company's financial activities.

Cooking the Books

Given such flexibility, the opportunities for fraud are boundless.

For example, let's say the Widget Company is having a bad third quarter. Sales are down, but the CEO has vowed to keep profits—and the company's stock price—soaring. He goes to the sales manager and says, "Get me some big numbers to close out Q3—or you're fired."

The sales manager calls up a buddy at a big retailer. The sales manager says, "If you place an order for a million widgets this week, I'll ship them to your warehouse, where they can sit. After a month or so, I'll take back the unsold product. In exchange I'll give you a ten percent discount."

The retailer says, "You know I couldn't sell a million widgets in a *year*, much less a month!"

The sales manager says, "I know. Look, I'll hire you as a consultant. Pay you five thousand dollars cash to 'consult.' Just take the damn widgets, won't you?"

The next day, the sales manager reports to the CEO that a big sale of one million widgets has been made. In the company's ledgers, the value of the sale is posted at ten million dollars. Good news! The investors will be happy and the stock price will stay sky-high.

No one will notice when, a month later, nine hundred and ninety-nine thousand widgets arrive back at the Widget Company's warehouse. The supposed income from the sale is still on the books, to be shoved around from column to column until only a professional forensic accountant could figure out the source of the fraud.

This is not a hypothetical story. It's a common fraud called "channel stuffing." Here's a true case.

Sunbeam Fills Its Ledgers With Fraud

In 1996, Albert "Chainsaw" Dunlap was brought in as chairman and CEO of Sunbeam Corporation, the venerable consumer goods manufacturer whose earnings and stock price had been in sharp decline for two years. Sunbeam needed a fast turnaround and he was the guy who could do it.

Investors were ecstatic that "Rambo in Pinstripes" had arrived to save the company, and Sunbeam's stock leaped nearly fifty percent the day he was hired to run the company. Sunbeam's fortunes seemed to quickly improve. Dunlap eliminated excess products and closed factories and warehouses. He eliminated half the company's 12,000 employees and consolidated Sunbeam's six headquarters into one facility in Delray Beach, Florida—which happened to be Dunlap's primary residence.

"We are winning in every aspect of our business," Dunlap told analysts in the conference call announcing 1997 earnings. "What an amazing year we had."

The exit strategy was to find a buyer for the company, which would have enabled Dunlap to make millions from selling his stock and cashing in his options. But no buyer stepped forward.

Having slashed expenses but with no buyer in sight, Dunlap was forced to do something that he'd never done before: increase sales. There was no other way to keep investors happy and the stock price rising.

Unfortunately, Dunlop had zero experience in actually building the value of a company through sales. His solution was to unload as much product as possible, claim the shipments as sales, and book the anticipated revenue as income. Dunlap began to engage in "bill and hold" contracts in which Sunbeam products were purchased by retailers at steep discounts and then held at third-party warehouses for delivery later. Basically, he was stealing sales from future quarters and cramming them into current ones. By booking these sales before the goods were delivered, in 1997 Dunlap inflated Sunbeam's revenues by eighteen percent.

Amazingly, the strategy was technically not illegal, and if you inspected the company's ledgers the numbers seemed legitimate. But disaster was just around the corner. Channel stuffing means the inventory sitting in the warehouses of wholesalers hasn't really been sold, and will inevitably either sit there for months or come back as returns. If you've got a million toasters in warehouses in September, retailers will still be selling them in January, which means that your wholesalers won't order any more. This means that you won't sell any toasters in January. You've glutted the pipeline with product and you have to wait for the backlog to clear.

Dunlap defended the practice, saying that it was an effort to "better meet surges in demand" and "extend the selling season."

To maintain growth, in early 1998 Dunlap boldly announced three acquisitions: Coleman, the camping equipment company; First Alert, the smoke-alarm company; and Mr. Coffee, the coffeepot maker. The acquisitions were accomplished by taking on debt, which required a high valuation of Sunbeam stock.

Investors were impressed by the ambitious move, and within two days Sunbeam's stock jumped to an all-time high of $52 per share.

Analysts became suspicious when they discovered certain seasonal items were being sold at higher volume than normal for the time of year. For example, they observed that sales of barbeque grills were high in the fourth quarter, which is an unusual time of year for grills to be sold. They noticed that while electric blankets typically sell well in the cold-weather fourth quarter, there were huge increases in sales in the warm-weather third quarter.

On April 3, 1998, Sunbeam stock was downgraded and the price began to fall. A few weeks later a class action lawsuit was filed naming both Sunbeam Corporation and CEO Dunlap as defendants. The lawsuit alleged that Sunbeam and Dunlap had violated the Securities and Exchange Act of 1934 by "cooking the books" and misrepresenting and omitting material information concerning the business operations, sales, and sales trends of the company. The lawsuit also alleged that the motivation for artificially inflating the price of the common stock was to enable Sunbeam to complete millions of dollars of debt financing in order to acquire Coleman, First Alert, and Signature Brands.

The fraud was unraveling. By early June, *Barron's* published an article noting that Sunbeam had negative operating cash flow in 1997 and suggesting that all the company's profits had come from questionable accounting maneuvers.

In 2001, Sunbeam filed for bankruptcy protection. On May 15 of that year, the Securities and Exchange Commission accused Albert Dunlap of fraud. It was revealed that some of the fraudulent transactions were uncovered by the company's outside auditors, who asked Sunbeam to change its financial statements. The company's management refused to make most of the requested changes, and—amazingly—the auditors agreed to certify the financial statements anyway, having been convinced that the challenged numbers were not material and therefore did not have to be corrected.

The following year Sunbeam emerged from bankruptcy, was bought by Jarden Corp., and today is a reputable consumer brand.

This story—and many more like it—reveal that just because a company keeps official-looking ledgers, and even has them reviewed by an outside auditor, doesn't mean that the books don't contain dark secrets.

Opportunity 3: Deliver on Consistent Financial Control

As the complexity and reach of commerce increased, the need to record, review and report on the state of value creation, capture and transfer via ledgers un-

locked mankind's greed. The need to cooperate for the betterment of all is now at risk of being stolen by one. Commerce is in a state of fearing fraud, often committed by those already with power, and wealth.

4. The Flow of Wealth

No one can deny that the invention of the ledger book and double-entry bookkeeping was a great leap forward in the development of our ability to organize ourselves into large groups—corporations and partnerships—for the purpose of sustained trade, manufacturing, and wealth creation. It took us through the Mercantile Age and the Industrial Age. And now, as we find ourselves deep into the Information Age, it's time to take stock of our progress—or lack thereof—in our common efforts to achieve better health, longer lives, equitable distribution of wealth, and political and cultural empowerment for all people.

There can be no doubt that in the grand scheme of things, corporations have been wildly successful in amassing wealth for their owners. If you measure a public company's wealth by its market valuation—which fluctuates over time—it's clear that the biggest multinational corporations have amassed more stored value than the gross domestic products of many nations.

For example, based on the Financial Times Global 500 rankings, as of this writing the market value of the world's wealthiest corporation, Apple Inc., is $617 billion. Following are Alphabet (Google) ($531 billion), Microsoft ($483 billion), Berkshire Hathaway ($401 billion), and Amazon ($356 billion).

Looking at national gross domestic product, it's no surprise that China, the United States, and the European Union—the homes of most of the world's biggest corporations—each post GDPs approaching $20 trillion.

But look further down the list. At #38 is Belgium, with a GDP of $508 billion—less than Apple! Sweden comes next at $498 billion. Switzerland, Venezuela, Austria, Norway, all trail behind the biggest corporations. Denmark, which at #61 posts a GDP of $264 billion, would not even make the list of top ten global corporations.

On its face, perhaps there's nothing intrinsically wrong with this. If a corporation is successful and provides what people want and need, then is there any reason why it shouldn't scale up? An advocate of a pure free market system would say, "There's no reason why a successful company can't grow to its optimum size. Larger size equals greater efficiency, lower costs, more jobs, and more products."

With size and wealth comes power. Not even the most ardent free market partisan could deny that the economic power of multinational corporations is significant. Vast lobbying resources and revolving doors to lawmakers enable corporations to wield outsized influence over international institutions and governments to help to advance their own interests. And while big corporations operate across borders, laws are still primarily nationally based. To date, there is almost no legally binding international regulation of corporations. Attempts to hold corporations to account at an international level are generally voluntary and therefore unenforceable.

To many people, there can be problems with huge corporations that control and, in some cases, hoard vast wealth. Take Apple, for example. Billions of people around the world use and love Apple products, from computers to phones to digital music. And in return, Apple has been very good at vacuuming cash from its customers and stashing it away. As CNBC reported in January 2017, in the fiscal first quarter Apple's enormous cash hoard stood at $246.09 billion, up $8.49 billion from the previous quarter. If Apple's cash pile were its own public company, it would be the thirteenth largest in the world. According to the figures published in the *CIA World Factbook*, Apple could, in theory, take its cash and buy everything produced by Finland, or Ecuador, or New Zealand, or Kenya, or Cuba, or a whole host of smaller nations.

Where is all the Apple cash stored?

For tax reasons, Apple keeps most of its cash outside the United States. President Donald Trump and members of Congress have pledged to change rules on repatriation of cash stored overseas, which could make it easier for Apple to spend some of the money on acquisitions without taking a major tax hit. Apple CEO Tim Cook told CNBC, "Repatriation is front and center. That is good for the country and Apple."

Time will tell if that happens.

The Widening Wealth Divide

Historically, wealth gaps are nothing new. It's human nature for wealth to flow towards people in leadership positions, whether kings or CEOs. In the very old days, people had two ways of amassing wealth. The first was by brute force. The biggest caveman in the valley took what he wanted and bashed in the head of anyone who argued. Conquerers led armies and seized the wealth of subjugated lands—goods, food, domestic animals, gold, and human captives as slaves. Bands of outlaws attacked trading caravans or ships and took what they could haul away. Nations invaded other nations and seized from the vanquished their raw materials, energy supplies, wealth, arable land, and human labor.

Building wealth by force can happen on a big scale. Historians Arnold J. Toynbee and James Burke have argued that the economy of the Roman Empire was a *Raubwirtschaft* or "plunder economy" based on looting existing resources rather than producing anything new. The Empire relied on wealth plundered from conquered territories and a system of tax collection and tribute imposed upon their inhabitants. Wealthy Romans profited hugely from the perpetual war economy, while subjugated populations worked as virtual slaves to sustain the Empire's military might. The Empire's vast slave trade was a cornerstone of its economy, with most slaves acquired as war captives, to be sold as property to the Roman citizenry.

The seizing of wealth by force has happened as recently as March 2014, when the Russian Federation "annexed"—a polite word for covertly invaded and took over—the peninsula of Crimea. The move gave Russia access to oil and gas reserves potentially worth trillions of dollars, and altered the route along which the South Stream pipeline would be built to the Black Sea, saving Russia time, money, and engineering challenges. In addition, Russian President Vladimir Putin, who ordered the seizure, was apparently worried that Russia would lose her strategically important naval base in Sevastopol, on the western tip of Crimea.

Being a supreme monarch has traditionally represented a ticket to immense wealth. The wealthiest human being in all of history—after adjusting for inflation—was an obscure ruler of the late medieval African empire of Mali, which covered modern day Ghana, Timbuktu and Mali. At the time of his death in 1331, Mansa Musa I had a personal net worth estimated at $400 billion in today's dollars. Born in 1280, Musa inherited his throne through the Malian practice of appointing a deputy to serve when the reigning king to made his pilgrimage to Mecca. Musa was appointed deputy of the king before him, who reportedly left on his journey and never returned, leaving Musa to ascend the throne. The source of Musa's vast wealth? At the time, Mali was the source of more than half the world's supply of salt and gold. For every gold nugget or pound of salt shipped out of the empire, Musa received his cut.

Even today, being a monarch is a good-paying position. Until he passed away in 2016, King Bhumibol Adulyadej of Thailand was the wealthiest royal, worth $30 billion. His reign lasted sixty-four years, and the bulk of his wealth came from his vast real estate holdings throughout Thailand, which he inherited. His anointed successor, Crown

Prince Vajiralongkorn, will likewise inherit the family fortune. The royal accounts are managed by the Crown Property Bureau (CPB), a secretive tax-exempt institution that issues no annual report and answers only to the king, whose investment strategy is confidential. There cannot be any doubt the CPB keeps sets of account books, but they are not open to inspection. No one outside the CPB and the royal family sees them.

Meanwhile, the average annual salary for an ordinary Thai citizen who must work for a living is approximately $15,000 a year.

This brings us to the focus of this chapter, which is not so much the absolute wealth of people at the top, but the difference between living at the narrow top of the pyramid and barely surviving at the broad base.

There has always been an income gap between rich and poor. There probably always will be. The question is, how wide is the gap? And does the gap represent an inherent unfairness in the system, or are those at the bottom—as many who admire thinkers like Ayn Rand might assert—are simply lazy, unimaginative, or unconcerned with acquiring wealth?

It's a big topic. If you Google "the income gap," you'll get nearly ten million results.

The twenty-first century has ushered in a new period of lavish pay packages for CEOs of big corporations. According to recent studies, over that three-decade period, pay for chief executives has risen over one hundred times faster than worker pay. The paychecks of workers have failed to keep up with productivity gains in the workplace, and the minimum wage has failed to keep up with the buying power it once had. Meanwhile, minimum wage "burger flipping" jobs are becoming more prevalent, further depressing wages for low-income workers. Tax rates for the wealthy have fallen, which adds up to the fact that while the wealthy have experienced a solid recovery from the Great Recession, middle- and low-income Americans have largely been left behind.

It's not just income that matters, but wealth. Income refers to money received by a person or household over some period of time. It includes wages, salaries, dividends, and cash assistance from the government. Wealth refers to the value of assets held by a person or household at a single point in time. These assets may include financial holdings, savings, and real estate holdings. Wealth can be seen as the length of time that a person or family could maintain their current lifestyle without receiving compensation for performing additional work.

You can have significant wealth without a huge income. You can also have a high income but little wealth. For example, a family's expenses—the jumbo mortgage payment, the children's private schools, payments on new cars, student loans, luxury clothing, and the vacation home—add up. The total cost of indulging can be equal to the family's yearly income. Some families live paycheck to paycheck, despite their huge annual salaries.

When it comes to wealth—meaning a household's total assets, such as savings, value stored in a house, pensions, or other sources of money, minus anything it owes—there is growing inequality. The difference between wealth held by the top one percent at the top of the pyramid and the ninety-nine percent at the base has widened to levels not seen since the Roaring Twenties.

Opportunity 4: Address The Trust Gap

Large-scale cooperation, organization, coordination and recording of value created benefits way beyond survival of the species. We consequentially created the ability to amass wealth in a centralized manner, creating side effects such as the wealth and income gap. The wealth gap and the income gap have been joined by yet another kind of consequential disparity—the trust gap.

5. The Trust Gap

It's not only an income gap that we're facing—it's a gap in trust. Increasingly, the average citizen has a lack of faith in large corporations and government.

Trust can be measured. Edelman is a leading global communications marketing firm based in New York and Chicago. Published in 2013, their *Edelman Trust Barometer* is their thirteenth annual exploration of corporate trust and the largest survey of its kind. They surveyed more than 31,000 respondents in twenty-six markets around the world and measured their trust in institutions, industries, and leaders. The results show that of types of people, CEOs and government officials are at the bottom of the heap, with 42% and 36% ratings, respectively. Of types of companies, banks and financial services are likewise at the bottom, with only 50% of respondents rating them well on Edelman's nine-point scale. "We're clearly experiencing a crisis in leadership," said Richard Edelman, CEO of Edelman, in a statement. "Business and governmental leaders must change their management approach and become more inclusive, by behaving more transparently and seeking the input of employees, consumers, and activists along with traditional academics, and adapting to their feedback."

In an article written in 2015 for *The Economist*, he also said, "For the first time since the Great Recession, half the countries we survey have fallen into the 'distruster' category (that is, their overall level of trust, among the informed public, is below fifty percent). This is directly linked to the failure of key institutions to provide answers or leadership in response to events such as the refugee crisis, data breaches, China's stock market downturn, Ebola in west Africa, the invasion of Ukraine, the FIFA bribery scandal, VW's manipulation of emissions data, massive corruption at Petrobras, and exchange-rate manipulation by the world's largest banks."

In 2006, *Forbes* published an article entitled "The Economics of Trust." The author, Tim Hartford, asked the reader to imagine a world where in even the simplest of transactions there was no trust. In his story, you go to the corner store to buy a carton of milk. The refrigerator where the milk is stored is locked. You must persuade the shopkeeper to open the case and take out a carton of milk. Then you argue over whether you're going to pay him the money before he hands over the milk, or whether he is going to give you the milk and then you pay. Finally you manage to arrange an elaborate simultaneous exchange.

Actually, this scenario will be familiar to anybody who has patronized a liquor store in a low-income neighborhood. There you might be required to stand in line at a window with a thick steel screen. When it's your turn you tell the cashier what you want, and then you wait while he takes the bottle off the shelf. You pay, and then he hands you the paper bag through the window. There is very little trust.

Similar rules apply at jewelry stores, where the inventory is kept inside glass cases, and if you want to see a ring or a brooch, the salesperson must retrieve it and hand it to you, and then watch you like a hawk while you try it on.

Fortunately, in everyday life we make routine transactions with a high degree of trust. You can go to the supermarket, fill up your cart with merchandise, and then leisurely push your cart to the cashier. While the store may be discreetly watching you, the general tone is one of trust. We learned early on as a species that we have to trust each other to transact with each other, and I believe in the cases where we cannot systematically manufacture or provide evidence of trust, we source this trust from our gut in order to continue to corporate, organize, and govern.

Hartford pointed out that while being able to trust people is a nice convenience, many economists are starting to believe that a deeply rooted culture of trust, or lack of it, has much more profound implications for national development. They say that trust is about more than whether you can fill your shopping cart without the store detective trailing you; it may be responsible for the difference between the richest countries and the poorest.

"If you take a broad enough definition of trust, then it would explain basically all the difference between the per capita income of the United States and Somalia," said Steve Knack, a senior economist at the World Bank to *Forbes*. Without a solid foundation of trust between individuals, institutions, and government agencies, even the simplest transactions become difficult. Trust enables people to do business with each other, and commerce creates wealth.

Enron: The Poster Child for Mistrust

Walk down any street and ask random passersby if they know the name "Enron," and just about every one of them will reply, "Of course I do! That's the giant company that went bankrupt because it was run by a bunch of crooks." The name has entered popular lore because the immense scandal was so outrageous that it seemed almost unbelievable. Just like "Benedict Arnold" is a synonym for "traitor," "Enron" is now a synonym for "corporate duplicity."

Enron was a huge global energy company that grew at a phenomenal rate. Between 1996 and 2000, the company reported an amazing increase in sales from $13.3 billion to $100.8 billion. As would be the case in any company, these numbers were generated and reported by company managers. At the time, the company appeared to be brilliantly managed. In August 2000, Enron shares reached their all-time high of ninety dollars per share. Investors were delighted.

Sixteen months later, on December 2, 2001, Enron declared bankruptcy. The next day the company laid off four thousand workers. An employee later revealed that Enron had paid $55 million in "retention bonuses" to top managers and executives just before going belly-up.

How could the bubble have gotten so big—and then exploded—so quickly?

The answer was in the company's incomprehensible ledgers.

The scandal was rooted in the creation of phony business structures and accounting treatments that were so complicated that, to this day, highly skilled forensic accountants and investigators have difficulty deciphering them. The goal was simple: to manipulate the corporate ledgers to give the appearance of robust revenues and minimal losses. In turn, this would foster investor confidence and keep the price of Enron stock rising. To meet their goal, the conspirators—led by CEO Jeffrey Skilling and CFO Andrew Fastow—inflated revenues, hid liabilities, and concocted a vast web of offshore "limited liability special purpose entities" with names like Condor, Egret, Whitewing, Raptor, and Trakya. From an accounting standpoint, these shell companies were treated not as entities that were part of Enron, but as investments. This "off-balance-sheet" approach enabled Enron to shift revenues and expenses to meet and exceed the expectations of Wall Street analysts and rating agencies, and artificially inflate the value of Enron stock.

But surely there must have been someone who could have spotted the deception? Yes, there was.

In a legitimate company, the numbers reported by managers to investors are verified by the company's independent auditor. In turn, the work of the auditor is overseen by the company's board of directors, which is made up of presumably honest and objective people who have the best interests of investors at heart. This three-legged system—management, auditors, and directors—is designed to give confidence to investors, who are putting their money at risk when they buy stock. They need to trust that they're getting an accurate picture of the company's performance.

Let's look at Enron's auditor, the agency that was supposed to detect and report irregularities in the books.

Enron's auditor was the accounting giant Arthur Andersen, and specifically its Houston office. As the scandal unfolded, government investigators uncovered a pattern of self-dealing and the failure of Arthur Andersen's Houston office to recognize and correct serious problems in Enron's books. One reason why the auditors turned a blind eye was a conflict of interest over the massive consulting fees paid to them by Enron. During 2000, Arthur Andersen earned $25 million in audit fees plus an additional $27 million in consulting fees, representing nearly one third of the revenues generated by Andersen's Houston office. The auditor's misleading reports and lack of rigor in reviewing Enron's special entities, revenue statements, derivatives, and other accounting practices were the result of the firm's priority being fee collection rather than maintaining high professional standards. They saw the ledgers and, to keep the Enron money flowing, chose to ignore suspicious or incomprehensible entries.

How about the Enron board of directors? Why didn't they step in to straighten out the books?

On paper, Enron had a respected board of directors and a capable audit committee comprised predominantly of outsiders with significant ownership stakes. But as with Arthur Anderson, there was a lot of money at stake. Enron directors were highly paid for their services and financially tied to the company. In 2001, the average Enron director was paid nearly $400,000 in cash and stock, using the value of Enron stock on the date of its annual meeting. The higher the stock price, the bigger the paycheck.

On January 19, 2002, Reed Abelson in *The New York Times* wrote an article entitled, "Enron's Collapse: The Directors— One Enron Inquiry Suggests Board Played Important Role."

"There is increasing evidence that Enron's board," he wrote, "composed of many prominent and financially sophisticated people, was actively involved in crucial decisions that may have led to the company's downfall. The directors appear to have played a significant role in overseeing the partnerships at the center of Enron's collapse."

You can have all the account books and ledgers you want, but if someone is determined to render them pointless through dazzling sleight of hand, they can quickly destroy trust. One irony of this story is that Enron's code of ethics was very strong. But it was just words on paper, rather than something practiced in real life. And long before the scandal confirmed the perception, people on the outside referred to the company as "the Crooked E," based not just on its hulking logo, but on its reputation in the marketplace. The big losers were the thousands of Enron employees tossed into the street, as well as Enron's faithful shareholders, who lost $74 billion in the four years before the company's bankruptcy.

So Many Ways to Commit Fraud

Wherever you combine human frailty, money, and secrecy, you're going to have at least a trust gap, and at worst massive fraud. From massive schemes like Enron and Bernard Madoff to petty skimming from the account of the local gas station, fraud in business is persistent and costly. According to a report by the Association of Certified Fraud Examiners, nearly half of all small businesses experience fraud at some point in their business lifecycle. Such episodes cost these organizations an average of $114,000, which for a small business can be crippling. Worse, such fraud is usually committed by an employee who seems loyal.

A person who wants to manipulate an organization's books or otherwise commit fraud has many ways to do it. Here are just a few.

General Ledger Fraud

As we saw at Enron, corporate ledgers can be very complex, and in big companies there may be very few people who have the expertise to understand them. While many employees may have working knowledge of the accounts they access daily, they may have little familiarity with the other parts. It's like an auto mechanic who knows how to fix the engine of the car but doesn't know anything about bodywork. Fiscal insiders may have exclusive access to accounts that make it easy for them to move funds between accounts. For example, an employee with the authority to create an accounts payable record for a vendor could also create a phony company in the system, issue payments to that company, and take the money for themselves.

Here's an example. From 1983 to 2012, Rita A. Crundwell was the appointed comptroller and treasurer of the city of Dixon, Illinois, and the perpetrator of what is believed to be the largest municipal fraud in American history. She was fired in April 2012 after it was revealed that she had embezzled $53.7 million from the city over twenty-two years. She pleaded guilty to her crimes and was sentenced to nearly twenty years in prison.

Her scheme was simple. It began on December 8, 1990, when, using her authority as treasurer, she opened a secret bank account named Reserve Sewer Capital Development Account (RSCDA), making it appear to be a city account.

She was the only signatory. She directed city revenues to be deposited into another account called the Capital Development Fund, while at the same time she created false state invoices. To pay them, she wrote checks from the fund payable to "Treasurer," which she would deposit into the RSCDA account. For twenty-two years, Crundwell stole an average of $5 million per year from the city.

For most of her tenure as comptroller, Crundwell had blanket authority over the city's accounts, to which very few other city employees had access. She explained the chronic cash shortfalls by claiming the state was regularly late in paying the city its share of tax revenue. It was a scheme that should have been easily detected, but the city's outside auditors were lax and signed off on Crundwell's financial statements without digging deeper.

How was Crundwell caught? She went on a long vacation, and a city clerk who was filling in for her discovered the fraudulent account and called the FBI.

Identity Theft

Another increasingly prevalent internal fraud scheme in financial institutions is the theft of ID data of customers.

In September 2016, Wells Fargo, the second-largest U.S. bank, was accused by state and federal regulators of encouraging its employees to access customers' personal information, and in some cases forge data, to subscribe those unwitting customers to products, including credit cards, that generated both commissions for salespeople and revenue for the bank. Prosecutors say an astounding two million spurious deposit and credit card accounts were opened without customers' knowledge.

This widespread campaign of fraud at Wells Fargo may represent one of the most massive examples of organized identity theft ever recorded. And when anyone examined the account ledgers of the bank, they wouldn't have seen anything out of place—because ledgers don't record the intent, or lack of intent, of the customer.

Wells Fargo agreed to pay $100 million to the Consumer Financial Protection Bureau as well as other fines. The enforcement actions against Wells Fargo will likely now cause regulators to look more closely at what governance structures are in place to prevent abuse and how banks incentivize sales associates.

Account Takeover

Account takeover occurs when someone gains unauthorized access to one or more of a customer's online accounts. While it usually involves an external attack, it can involve employees acting in collusion with outsiders. A bank employee may sell a customer's PIN and account number to an external perpetrator, change the address for the account, and request a new check card. The employee may open a deposit account for a customer and later set up online banking on the account without the customer's knowledge. The employee may then steal from the account or give the online credentials to an external perpetrator, who can use them to siphon money from the account.

Collusion With Outsiders

An insider can collude with an outside fraudster. For example, in 2012 a former loan officer named Jamie Lee Lawler, of Phoenix, Arizona, pleaded guilty to charges related to a mortgage fraud scheme and charges of bankruptcy fraud, wire fraud, mail fraud, and bank fraud in two separate indictments. Authorities said Lawler (interesting last name for someone who side stepped the law, LOL) used her position as a loan officer to carry out a $40 million mortgage fraud scheme, and that "after she was charged in the mortgage fraud case, she continued to commit egregious financial crimes."

According to Lawler's plea agreement, from January 2005 through December 2007, Lawler and others conspired to commit mortgage fraud by using unqualified straw buyers to purchase properties, knowing that the straw buyers did not intend to live in the homes or be responsible for the loan payments.

Lawler would obtain mortgage financing to purchase homes in the names of the sham buyers by submitting faked mortgage loan applications and altering documents such as bank statements to misrepresent the straw buyers' assets, income, and other qualifying information. Based on the false information regarding the buyers' ability to qualify for loans, lenders issued loans that exceeded the homes' sales prices. Once the funds were obtained from the lenders and the house bought, the extra proceeds, known as "cash-back," were funneled into bank accounts that Lawler controlled.

Countrywide and other lenders issued more than $38 million in loans based on the fraudulent applications, said the FBI, with about $8.7 million going to Lawler and other conspirators.

Common signs of accounting irregularities include:

- General ledger entries with transaction descriptions that are incomplete or nonsensical.

- Insiders, or their interests, frequently appearing on transaction suspense item listings, but not on the "updated" version that is presented to the board of directors or to examiners.

- Employees accessing accounts that are unusual for the scope of their job.

- Bank account reconcilements that are not current or that fail to describe the status of outstanding items.

Double Check Fraud

This is a very simple variety of accounting fraud in which the accounts payable employee writes two checks each time they pay a bill—one for the vendor and one for themselves. For example, if the perpetrator had to pay $800 to Ajax Vendor, they would simultaneously write another check to themselves for $100 that would coded in the accounting system as "Ajax."

This is an example of low-level "bleeding" that can pass unnoticed by a business owner or lazy auditor. Even if the owner is regularly looking at the financial statements and the bills look a little high, they might seem reasonable. But this kind of slow-drip fraud can add up quickly.

In every case, the fraud happens because someone wants to steal, and to both *accomplish* the theft and *cover it up* the organization's accounts are muddied or falsified. Too often there's a limit to the doggedness and determination of human auditors to uncover fraud. If the company seems healthy and nothing jumps out as looking egregious, then too many auditors are content to slap an "approved" sticker on the ledger and close the book. This tendency becomes more pronounced under two conditions: when the accounts are extraordinarily complex, as was the case with Enron, or when the people keeping the accounts appear to be beyond reproach, as was the case with Rita Crundwell and Bernie Madoff. Too often we human beings don't want to see that our trust has been sadly misplaced, and the consequences can often be costly.

Opportunity 5: Restore Trust and Transparency

The state of commerce today is massively untrusted. Most of the breaches occur where there is little or no transparency or accountability in the recording of the creation, capture, or transfer of value. In and some very large cases, the breaches occur in spite of excessive and redundant layers of transparency and accountability. But we have the data, why can't we stop this?

6. Big Data, Big Problems

Corporations—both for-profit and non-profit—can be very large and complex entities.

When measured by the number of employees, the world's largest organizations are currently the U.S. Department of Defense (3.2 million people on the payroll) and the People's Liberation Army of China (2.3 million). These are both military organizations with rigid hierarchical structures and very little transparency, which means that we're not going to spend time discussing them.

Number three on the list is Walmart, with 2.3 million on the payroll, which makes it roughly the size of the Chinese Army. It's also a publicly traded company, which at least in theory provides for a high level of transparency. It's followed by McDonald's, with 1.9 million employees including franchisees.

The Catholic Church

Before we discuss Walmart, you may be wondering about the Catholic Church, which, after all, was the first global organization in human history. In terms of its internal structure, the Church is organized in a worldwide hierarchy under the pope, the Bishop of Rome (Holy See), based in Vatican City. Around the world, within each nation or group of smaller nations, the Church is further organized into local hierarchies. National Conferences of bishops coordinate local policy within each nation. Archbishops and bishops administer individual dioceses, and are responsible for the ordination, appointment, and supervision of parish priests and the oversight of all church affairs within their diocese. In general, in matters of policy the Catholic Church is extremely hierarchical, while the day-to-day administration is extremely decentralized.

The Vatican itself has two main entities—the Holy See, which governs the Catholic Church, and the Vatican City State, which governs Vatican City. There is also *the Istituto per le Opere di Religione* (Institute for the Works of Religion), commonly known as the IOR or Vatican Bank. This is a private bank situated inside Vatican City. It's run by a Board of Superintendence, which in turn reports to a supervisory commission of cardinals and the pope.

While much of the inner workings of the Church are shrouded in secrecy, we do know how many people are employed by the Church. The Church publishes statistics in the form of the *Pontifical Yearbook 2016 and the Annuarium Statisticum Ecclesiae 2014: dynamics of a Church in transformation, 05.03.2016.* The *Yearbook* says that Church membership at the end of 2014 was 1.272 billion, which is 17.8% of the world population. As for people who receive some sort of Church paycheck, at the end of 2014 the Church said it employed 465,595 ordained clergy, while non-ordained ministers included 3,157,568 catechists (teachers), 367,679 lay missionaries, and 39,951 lay ecclesial ministers. In addition, there are "Catholics who have committed to religious or consecrated life instead of marriage or single celibacy, as a state of life or relational vocation, numbering 54,559 male religious, and 705,529 women religious." Presumably, these numbers refer to those whom most people call "monks" and "nuns." So the total number of people who in some way derive their livelihood from the Church approaches five million.

The Catholic Church is also very wealthy. The problem is that no one outside the Vatican knows exactly *how* wealthy because the Church ledger books are secret. As an exempt religious organization, in regard to its finances the Catholic Church is required to answer to no higher civil authority. While around the globe national laws vary, in the United States, religious institutions, including synagogues, mosques, mandirs, and churches, are required to file neither a form 1023, which grants tax exemption to nonprofits, nor a form 990, an annual return report required of federally tax-exempt organizations. The Church files no income taxes and, at least until 2015, released no annual report.

When it comes to its account books and bank balances, it's extraordinarily opaque. If the Church weren't built on the fervent faith of its members, the trust gap would be as wide as the Grand Canyon.

From Rome there has been some acknowledgement that perhaps the Church needs to become more transparent with its finances, or at least more businesslike.

In December 2014, the *Catholic Herald*, based in London, published this interesting item under the headline, "We've discovered hundreds of millions of euros off the Vatican's balance sheet, says cardinal."

Sure enough, Cardinal George Pell, the cardinal charged with sorting out the Roman Curia's financial affairs, wrote that Vatican reformers had discovered hundreds of millions of euros that did not appear on the balance sheet of the Holy See. (The administrative unit of the Holy See is called the Roman Curia, which assists the pope in governing the Catholic Church.) But this was good news, because the windfall meant that the Vatican's finances were "healthier than they first appeared."

He wrote, "In fact, we have discovered that the situation is much healthier than it seemed, because some hundreds of millions of euros were tucked away in particular sectional accounts and did not appear on the balance sheet. It is another question, impossible to answer, whether the Vatican should have much larger reserves."

It must be nice to discover millions of euros that you didn't realize you owned.

The goal of this discussion is not to denigrate the Catholic Church and its over one billion faithful followers. The point is to remind ourselves that when you combine great wealth, great secrecy, and human frailty, you get corruption. It's just as simple as that, and the formula applies to just about anyone, whether you wear an ecclesiastical collar or a power suit from Savile Row. Human beings are imperfect creatures, and temptation is difficult to resist, especially when you can commit your crimes in secret. It also serves to illustrate that even if people aren't intent on stealing, keeping secret ledgers and not knowing the location of every euro will inevitably lead to disorganization and waste.

Walmart

Let's return to the subject of publicly held corporations.

Headquartered in Bentonville, Arkansas, Wal-Mart Stores, Inc. employs of 2.3 million people. As of January 2017, Walmart had 11,695 stores and clubs in twenty-eight countries, operating under a total of sixty-three banners. Its governance is conventional and hierarchical. The board of directors consists of sixteen members, including two members of the Walton family as well as business executives including Kevin Systrom, CEO and co-founder of Instagram, and Marissa A. Mayer, president and CEO of Yahoo!, Inc. Top management includes the president and CEO of Wal-Mart Stores, Inc., and his (or her) four direct reports: the leaders of Walmart USA, Walmart International, Sam's Club, and Global Ecommerce and Technology. Under these five are twenty-nine senior managers—mostly executive vice presidents with a few C-levels. These include the financial people: executive vice president and treasurer, executive vice president and chief financial officer, senior vice president and controller.

Beneath them are various vice presidents and managers until you get to the individual stores, headed by a manager (Sam's Club) or two co-managers (the larger stores). Within the individual stores you have assistant managers, a support manager, supervisors, and lastly the cashiers, stockers, and sales associates.

In 2016, Walmart posted revenues of $485 billion.

How do they keep track of all that money?

It's not easy. While Walmart has generally been free of major accounting scandals—perhaps due in no small part to the relatively modest lifestyles pursued by the low-profile members of the Walton family—there have been problems.

In April 2013, Spencer Woodman wrote an article for *The Nation* that highlighted a persistent problem for the retailing behemoth—"shrink," which means the loss of inventory through theft, loss, or damage. Shrink is a problem for any retailer because if your ledger says you should have five hundred toasters on the shelves and a physical count reveals you've only got four hundred and eighty, that means you've paid for twenty toasters that suddenly don't exist and you can't sell. If you think shrink is a headache for the corner convenience store, imagine what it must be in a chain the size of a Walmart, with hundreds of thousands of items supervised by minimum-wage employees, and where profit margins are razor thin.

In his article entitled "Former Walmart District Manager Accuses Company of Widespread Inventory Manipulation," Woodman told the story of Sylvester Johnson, a district manager who oversaw eleven Walmart Supercenter stores in North Carolina. In 2009, the company fired him for allegedly giving orders to manipulate inventory counts, a claim Johnson denied. He also alleged—in an interview with

The Nation and in a federal discrimination lawsuit—that it was the company that engaged in persistent and widespread inventory manipulation.

Johnson asserted that the company's high command pressured him to hide losses due to shrinkage. The goal was for stores to appear more profitable than they really were. "We're talking about hiding tens or hundreds of millions of dollars in losses here—inflating the profits of a store, a district, a region, a division, and ultimately the entire company," Johnson told *The Nation*. Typically, the intended outcome of such a program of deception would be to illegally inflate the company's profit margins and therefore its stock price. This directly benefits top executives who are increasingly being paid with company stock.

This is not trivial. As Kim Souza reported for *Talk Business & Politics* (a news website that covers business, politics and culture in Arkansas) in February 2016, a small change in the price of Walmart stock can considerably fatten or shrink an executive's bank account. As she wrote in her article entitled "Walmart executive stock positions total $111 million amid share price rebound," on January 29, 2017 (the end of Walmart's fiscal 2016), in their personal and retirement accounts the company's top seven executives held more than 1.64 million shares of Walmart stock, with a market value of $109.238 million. For example, Wal-Mart Stores CEO Doug McMillon held 707,590 shares valued at $46.955 million. For every one dollar Walmart shares went up in price, McMillon's holdings increased by $707,590. Likewise, if the stock went down, he suffered an equivalent loss.

Meanwhile, district manager Sylvester Johnson said top management set shrinkage targets for Walmart Supercenter stores that were "not ethically attainable" and then used methods of "fear and intimidation" against him in an attempt to coerce him to meet those targets.

Walmart leadership denied the claims. The company terminated Johnson's employment in January of 2009 on the grounds that he instructed his subordinates to manipulate inventory accounting, which was precisely the practice that Johnson said he refused to participate in.

In 2015, Walmart appeared to recognize the problem with inventory shrinkage. In its second quarter report released August 18, 2015, astute analysts—who, because they're on the outside looking in, pore over these things as if they were modern-day Rosetta Stones—noted that the company acknowledged a problem. "Along with pharmacy headwinds," read the press release, "higher than expected ongoing shrink in Walmart U.S. will impact full year earnings per share (EPS) by approximately $0.11, including approximately $0.03 in the third quarter."

And Charles Holley, executive vice president and CFO, Wal-Mart Stores, Inc., added this personal sidebar:

"Operating profit will be pressured for the remainder of the year, due to continued investments in store associate wages and additional hours, as well as headwinds from pharmacy reimbursements and ongoing shrink, primarily in Walmart U.S."

If inventory shrink can be fudged with conventional accounting methods, think what you can do with taxes—or more precisely, concealing revenues from the prying eyes of the Internal Revenue Service.

The ability to transfer assets to other countries gives corporations like Walmart a powerful incentive to either *actually earn* profits offshore or make it *appear* they are earned offshore.

In June 2015, Bloomberg News reported that Wal-Mart Stores Inc. had more than $76 billion in assets stashed among a web of corporate units in offshore tax havens around the world—and these assets weren't listed in the company's annual report.

Reporters Jesse Drucker and Renee Dudley discussed a study researched by the United Food & Commercial Workers International Union and published by Americans for Tax Fairness, which charged that ninety percent of Walmart's overseas assets were controlled by subsidiaries in Luxembourg and the Netherlands, two popular corporate tax havens.

The Americans for Tax Fairness report stated, "Walmart has kept these tax-haven subsidiaries secretive by burying mention of their existence deep inside of SEC filings and financial documents filed by Walmart subsidiaries all around the world, only some of which are available to the public."

Opportunity 6: Deliver Data For Good

Is it legal? Probably. What is clear however is that big data does not mean trusted data or trusted people. I believe that the bigger the data, the more likely that disingenuous members of our species can tamper with said data, operating in dark corridors of mistrust.

7. Spreadsheets Need to be Disrupted

Given the ease with which organizations large and small are able to either conceal or falsify their books, you might think that digital technology would lead to more transparency in corporate accounting. After all, a physical ledger—an actual book of the kind used for hundreds of years—can be hidden while a fake duplicate is shown to auditors. In contrast (at least in theory), digital accounts can be endlessly replicated and shared, eliminating the secrecy of the physical ledger and closing the trust gap.

Yes and no.

There's no doubt the electronic spreadsheet—most popularly the Excel spreadsheet—has become ubiquitous. This is because it continues to meet the needs of companies for analyzing and reporting financial results, and providing actionable information for making decisions. Where data is continually changing and for complex calculations that require the use of cell functions, Excel is the most popular choice among people who crunch the numbers. Excel spreadsheets are used for tax computations, financial forecasting, budgeting, operational analysis, reporting, and much more.

Spreadsheets are also a good place to commit fraud.

Unlike physical books, which in the old days were written in pen and which would readily reveal evidence of tampering, with just a few clicks of a mouse digital spreadsheet data can be deliberately hidden or cleverly disguised, making it is easy for unscrupulous managers to manipulate the numbers for personal gain. On a larger scale, spreadsheet fraud—whether by altering truthful entries, hiding entries, or entering fake data—can a make a company appear to be worth more than it is. In the cases of Enron, Walmart, and many more, this was the goal of the perpetrators.

It's very possible for massive fraud to go undetected until the losses become enormous. In January 2008, the French bank Société Générale, one of the largest in Europe, lost approximately €4.9 billion closing out its positions over three days of trading. Apparently a "rogue employee" named Jérôme Kerviel had executed a series of "elaborate and fictitious transactions" that ultimately cost the company more than $7 billion, the biggest loss ever recorded in financial industry by a single trader.

Société Générale said it had no indication whatsoever that Kerviel, who joined the company in 2000, "had taken massive fraudulent directional positions in 2007 and 2008 far beyond his limited authority."

The bank added: "Aided by his in-depth knowledge of the control procedures resulting from his former employment in the middle-office, he managed to conceal these positions through a scheme of elaborate fictitious transactions."

As Diane Robinette wrote in her 2016 article "Stopping Spreadsheet Fraud" in *Corporate Compliance Insights*, without rigorous internal spreadsheet controls in place, changes can easily be made or data hidden, thus creating a false narrative. When formatting and organizing spreadsheets, for example, to create a gap between results, it's standard procedure to insert a blank column between two active columns. A row or column can be shrunk to near invisibility, making it easy to overlook. But even though the column seems to have no width, it's still a real column with real cells. Therefore, if a value is inadvertently or intentionally hidden within this cell, it will still be included in the calculations.

Another common way to conceal data is by merging cells. To make a spreadsheet easier to read, to hide irrelevant or sensitive data, or eliminate clutter, cells are often merged. While the ability to merge cells is supposed to provide greater efficiency for the ethical user, the feature can easily be used to hide data from overseers.

With the growing awareness that electronic spreadsheets, despite seeming to be more transparent by virtue of their ability to be duplicated and/or shared, thus putting more "eyes" on them, can be falsified as easily as an old-fashioned ledger book, software developers have taken steps to improve spreadsheet security and make it more difficult to either conceal or alter data, raising the level of trust.

The first step in managing spreadsheets across an organization is to carefully and methodically determine where risks may be hidden. "Spreadsheet management solutions"—that is, software programs designed to provide analysis and security—can provide enhanced insight into an organization's spreadsheets, regardless of how many exist or where they reside on a network. Such security solutions can provide insight into key metrics including what data has been changed and who made the changes; when the change was made; what employee (or even non-employee) has been working on a file; and how many people have worked on it over time. Having the capability to monitor and track who has access to a spreadsheet and what they've done over a defined period of time gives both leaders and overseers insight into whether users are adhering to company policies and to the law, as well allowing accountants to more easily identify potential risks.

In addition to locating misrepresented or hidden data within spreadsheets so that fraudulent activity is brought to light, as an added feature some solutions strive to keep human oversight failure out of the loop by allowing alerts to be automatically triggered if changes occur to key information categories such as shrink rates, the date when income was recognized, refunds given, or inventory levels. Such alerts, which can be as simple or detailed as necessary, can be tailored to meet an organization's particular criteria.

They serve as automated checks and balances to ensure both fraud and innocent mistakes are detected and corrected.

History is a Cycle of Disruptions

While these safeguards all very well and good, instead of transforming the status quo they add a new layer of complexity and expense to the existing accounting process, making the system increasingly cumbersome and loaded with "bells and whistles." But if you look back through history, the inevitable trend is for paradigms to start out simple and become progressively more complicated until a new, simple paradigm breaks through to replace what has come before. This is the cycle of innovation, which says that a new technology first emerges as a simple solution to a problem that's being solved by an older, more cumbersome solution; but, over time, as the shortcomings of the new solution are revealed and "improvements" are made, it become increasingly complex until a new, simpler paradigm emerges.

Consider the technology of the sailing ship. The basic idea is stunningly simple: You hoist some sort of wind-catching device on a mast, and *voilà*, you have a free source of energy to move your boat! To prehistoric people who were accustomed to powering their boats only with their own muscle energy, this development must have seemed amazing. Think about trade and warfare, and the incredible advantage an ancient society with sailboats would have over one equipped only with human-powered boats. People quickly got the hang of the new technology, and by about 3400 BCE the first sailing ships were in use on the River Nile in Egypt. They had a single mast with a square sail, which, when the wind was blowing in a favorable direction, could be used instead of oars. The Phoenicians took the new idea and ran with it, and with their sturdy seagoing cargo ships, called *hippoi*, they developed the ports of Sidon and Tyre and established thriving trade routes with cities around the Mediterranean coast. Riches flowed their way as they traded their manufactured products, including glassware and dyes, for linen, oils, ivory, and other goods.

For nearly three thousand years, wind power was the standard method of propulsion for ships large and small. But there were nagging drawbacks—principally the fact that the wind is both fickle and potentially violent. On the open ocean, you might be becalmed one day and hit by a hurricane the next. But perhaps the biggest problem is that big sailing ships require a lot of labor to operate. For example, one of the last big sailing vessels was the *Preußen* (often spelled *Preussen* in English). Built in 1902, the *Preußen* was a German steel-hulled ship with five masts, each carrying six square-rigged sails. That's a total of thirty sails that needed to be managed. Her length was 482 feet and she was designed to carry roughly 8,000 tons of nitrate or other bulk cargo. A sturdy ship, she was successfully used in the saltpeter trade with Chile, even setting speed records in the process. Due to her appearance, uniqueness, and excellent sailing characteristics, until her demise in 1910 seamen called her the "Queen of the Queens of the Seas."

The *Preußen* required a crew of forty-five men to haul her 8,000 tons of cargo at the mercy of the wind.

Fast-forward to the present day. *MS Ore Brasil* is a very large ore carrier owned by the Brazilian mining company Vale. The overall length of *Ore Brasil* is 1,188 feet, making her one of the longest ships currently on the seas. She has seven cargo holds with a combined net tonnage of 67,993. Propelled by a huge diesel engine, she sails (the old word is still used!) with a crew of thirty-three.

The basic technology of *Ore Brasil*—and every other modern cargo ship—is relatively simple and overcomes the liabilities of sail power. You build a huge ship, put a diesel engine in it, and go wherever you want, regardless of the weather. And because there are no complicated sails and rigging to manage, you can do this with a much smaller crew. With the *Preußen*, you could haul roughly 180 tons of cargo per crewmember. In contrast, the *Ore Brasil* hauls about 2,000 tons of cargo per crewmember.

The cycle of innovation introduced sail power to ancient people, which over time blossomed and matured until its growing complexity and inherent limitations opened the door for self-propelled ships using steam, diesel, and even nuclear power.

The point of this story—and there are countless similar examples throughout history—is that the cycle of innovation stipulates that new, simple technologies inevitably grow and become increasingly cumbersome until the next wave of new technologies and ideas supplant them. These disruptive new technologies face resistance before the tide turns and they become mainstream.

Opportunity 7: Get Out of Spreadsheet Hell

The spreadsheet is no longer effective at catering to the expanding complexity of commerce. We must adopt to embrace new customer types with artificial intelligence on the horizon, new marketplace with virtual and augmented reality on the horizon, and new trading partners

as smart devices come online. There is no debate that we need new tools, and new corporate models. Most of the progress we have seen is actually just wool.

8. The New Corporate Models Aren't So New

As we have discussed, the corporation as we know it today has been around since the seventeenth century—more than three hundred years. In all that time, it hasn't changed much. Lots of other things have evolved—steam and other types of engines have replaced sail power, and electronic spreadsheets have replaced the ancient ledgers. But the basic form of the corporation remains the same. We still have investors who buy ownership shares, boards of directors who provide oversight, and managers who run the day-to-day operations. We still have finance people who keep the books and auditors who check the work of the finance people. And we still have scandals created by every imaginable variety of malfeasance, whether by stupidity, greed, or criminal intent.

It's not that corporations are all terrible, just like sailing ships aren't all terrible. When they're successful, corporations are good at doing certain things.

They are good at responding to opportunities in the market. If there's a place on earth that needs refrigerators and has none, it's certain that a refrigerator salesman will be on the next plane, charged by his boss with opening a showroom in the neglected area.

You can argue that corporations are pretty good at providing jobs for people with various skill levels.

Corporations have shown themselves to be effective at product innovation. Apple isn't a federal program, it's a corporation, and it's spearheaded amazing advances in technology.

On the other hand, corporations have been, and still are, tremendously effective ways to concentrate wealth in the hands of the relatively few who have ownership. Witness Apple, with its cash hoard of $246.09 billion, mostly stashed in overseas accounts. Who owns this money? The corporation does, meaning all the stockholders. But the more important question is, who *controls* this money? Who can move it around and decide how to spend it? You can bet it's not the little old lady who owns a hundred shares of Apple stock. It's a handful of people in the C-suite in Cupertino, California.

Because of their size and complexity, corporations are fertile ground for buck-passing and obfuscation. For example, consider the fact that in the wake of the 2008 Great Recession, the number of Wall Street executives who have gone to jail for playing a part in the crisis is exactly *one*. (This highly unfortunate whipping boy is Kareem Serageldin, a senior trader at Credit Suisse, was convicted for inflating the value of mortgage bonds in his trading portfolio.) According to then-Attorney General Eric Holder, the reason for the lack of convictions was that corporate officials are increasingly skilled at erasing the trails of evidence that lead to their desks. As William D. Cohan wrote in *The Atlantic*, "Wall Street bankers make it their daily business to figure out ways to abide by the letter of the law while violating its spirit."

How about the information revolution? Wasn't that supposed to usher in a new era of transparency and trust?

Information technology has changed *commerce*, not the corporation. Its chief feature, the Internet, has revolutionized retail sales, and the way we buy products is very different now than it was even twenty years ago.

Instead of going to the neighborhood store or to the mall, you can buy anything online, from prepared dinners to automobiles to cheaper medications.

You can do your banking online, and execute investment trades.

You can find someone to date online, and after you've been married for a while you can go online and get legal advice on how to get divorced.

You can earn your college degree online, and then search for a job and apply for one, all without leaving your kitchen table.

If you own a business, your supply chain can be managed online. Let's say you own a string of hundreds of beverage machines located in shopping malls and public buildings. In the old days, on a regular basis your inventory people would have to drive in their service vans to each machine, open it up, count the number of cans of soda remaining, determine which were sold out, and replenish the supply. Today, each machine can be connected by the Internet to your headquarters, and the machine itself can provide real-time data on sales and inventory. It can tell you which cans of soda are cold and which ones are still warm. It can tell you at what times of day it's making the most sales, so you can devise strategies to boost sales during off-peak hours. This is the "Internet of things" (IoT), defined as the networking of physical devices, vehicles, buildings, and other items embedded with sensors, software, actuators, and network connectivity components that enable connected objects to collect and exchange data with each other or a central computer.

But underneath the heady excitement of the Information Age, the corporation lumbers along, unchanged.

In recent years we've seen the emergence of a handful of new corporations that, at first glance, seem to be new models. But are they really?

Uber

Headquartered in San Francisco, California, Uber Technologies Inc. is a transportation network company in which independent drivers use their own cars to ferry their passengers. Founded in 2009 by Garrett Camp and Travis Kalanick, the story is that on New Year's Eve in 2008, Camp spent eight hundred dollars hiring a private driver for himself and his friends. This expense made him think about ways to decrease the cost of black car services. He realized that sharing the cost with people could make it affordable, and his idea morphed into Uber. Now the company operates in 570 cities worldwide.

The attraction of Uber is that it eliminates the middleman of the traditional car-for-hire or taxi exchange—that is, the dispatcher. It's all about the technology. As the Uber website says, "Uber is a technology platform. Our smartphone apps connect driver-partners and riders."

It's a new technology that simplifies an existing industry, just like the Big Bang theory was simple solution to a host of vexing problems plaguing other theories. As economist Richard D. Wolff said on the David Pakman Show, Uber is following in the footsteps of preceding taxi services that started out in the United States over a century ago:

"Eventually these businesses were reined in by government after public outcry to make sure the taxis were safe and did not harm their customers. Uber is competing with licensed taxi drivers who are vetted and certified and have vehicles that are maintained for safety. Being unregulated allows Uber to charges less for the same service as taxis. Claims by Uber to have 'new technology' or 'shared value' or 'ridesharing' are merely public relation strategies."

Uber is a privately held company whose reported revenues in 2015 were $10.8 billion. Much of what we know about its finances comes from a set of internal documents that was leaked in August of 2015. As Artyom Dogtiev wrote in Businessofapps.com on September 5, 2016, "According to the leaked documents, currently Uber remains an unprofitable company. Back in 2014 GAAP losses (net revenue minus cost of revenue, operating expenses and other costs) totaled $671 million. In the first half of 2015 the losses increased 47% and reached $987.2 million.

Behind the outward appearance of populism, Uber is no different from any other classic privately held corporation.

According to a recent paper by Paolo Tasca, director at the Centre for Blockchain Technologies, and Mihaela Ulieru, president of The Impact Institute, Uber offers "nothing more than [a] two-sided platform business model," creating value exclusively for their owners "who control them."

They wrote, "To the novice, Uber-like networks seem to be decentralized. Yet while Uber runs on a 'smart' phone, it does so via a quite 'dumb' application (app), which links into a centralized platform, which is completely controlled by and supports the goals of the company. Centralized innovation means slow innovation. It also means innovation directed by the goals of a single company. Finally, it means single point of failure."

You'll note the word "blockchain" in the name of Tasca's organization. It also happens to be in the title of this book. In the pages ahead we'll be discussing how, in Tasca's view, blockchain technology can be used to transform a business like Uber from an old-fashioned corporation to something truly new and exciting.

As for Uber, what began as a very simple idea—so simple that many regulators instantly attacked it—quickly got mired down in increasing complexity. One of the most serious emerging points of contention is that in Uber's business model, its drivers are independent contractors, not employees. The difference, as any taxicab company knows, is huge. As the IRS says, "Generally, you must withhold income taxes, withhold and pay Social Security and Medicare taxes, and pay unemployment tax on wages paid to an employee. You do not generally have to withhold or pay any taxes on payments to independent contractors." Independent contractors are simpler to hire and fire, require minimal paperwork, and require no employer contribution to health or retirement plans.

The problem is that people who drive full time for Uber inevitably begin to think of themselves as employees, not independent contractors. Many of them have decided to sue.

As Classaction.com reported, "Uber class action lawsuits filed in numerous states challenge whether drivers for the ride-sharing company are independent contractors—as Uber claims—or employees, as many drivers assert."

As independent contractors who for tax purposes are given 1099 forms rather than W-2s, Uber drivers must pay their own job-related expenses including insurance, fuel, and vehicle maintenance. But they assert that the company treats them like employees and they should be classified as such, and therefore receive wage protections and other job-related benefits. Reclassifying drivers as W-2 employees could possibly force Uber to offer additional worker benefits such as health insurance, workers' compensation, and minimum wage. It would also give the company more control over its drivers, which it doesn't want but may have to accept.

The problem is not unique to Uber. As the US Treasury Department wrote in "Employers Do Not Always Follow Internal Revenue Service Worker Determination Rulings," published June 14, 2013, "The IRS estimates that employers misclassify millions of workers as independent contractors instead of employees, thus avoiding the payment of employment taxes. This problem adversely affects employees because the employer's share of taxes is not paid and the employee's share is not withheld."

To settle two class action lawsuits in California and Massachusetts, Uber offered $100 million in compensation. Under the agreement, Uber drivers would remain independent contractors, but be entitled to compensation. The settlement was rejected by U.S. District Judge Edward Chen, who argued the sum was far too small to settle a case that could result in $1 billion in penalties. At a hearing held on November 18, 2016, the judge stayed the case pending several appeals that Uber has filed challenging the court's rulings regarding Uber's arbitration clause.

Could Uber be organized differently? Yes—but more about that in the pages ahead.

Airbnb

Another company that has gotten a "buzz" of corporate progressivism is Airbnb, founded in 2008 after two San Francisco designers who had space to share hosted three travelers looking for a place to stay. Today, Airbnb is a global online marketplace and hospitality service, which matches property owners or "hosts" with customers who want to lease or rent short-term lodging such as hostel beds, vacation rentals, homestays, apartment rentals, or hotel rooms. The cost of lodging is set by the host. Like all hospitality services, Airbnb is a form of collaborative consumption and sharing.

The company does not own any lodging; it is only a broker, and in conjunction with every booking takes percentage service fees (commissions) from both guests and hosts. As of this writing, Airbnb boasts over three million lodging listings in 65,000 cities and 191 countries.

Airbnb is privately owned and has no shareholders. The Airbnb founding team acts as the key staff for Airbnb: Brian Chesky, co-founder and chief executive officer; Joe Gebbia, co-founder and chief product officer; and Nathan Blecharczyk, co-founder and chief technical officer. Other key executives include Laurence A. Tosi J.D., chief financial officer, and Chip Conley, head of global hospitality. Bloomberg, which is pretty good at uncovering financial information, doesn't list the names of the members of the board of directors or any committees. The only name associated with the board is Reid G. Hoffman of ProFounder Financial, Inc. As of March 13, 2017, Airbnb stated it did not have any specific plans to go public.

What's Airbnb worth? As *The Wall Street Journal* reported in March 2017, "according to a person familiar with the matter" the company closed its most recent funding round at

$3 billion, giving it a value of $31 billion, providing a comfortable cash cushion to stave off an initial public offering.

Technology Crossover Ventures and Google Capital led the

round, which included investments from existing shareholders Sequoia Capital and Andreessen Horowitz.

Since it was founded in 2008, Airbnb has raised over three billion dollars.

With the company's rise, the traditional hotel industry pushed back. According to the WSJ, a research report published by the American Hotel and Lodging Association called Airbnb a "professional short-term rental operation" rather than a "casual home-sharing service."

The big hotel chains, which had initially dismissed Airbnb, became increasingly concerned that investors had pegged Airbnb's value at $31 billion; in contrast, Marriott's market capitalization was $35 billion and Hilton's was $19 billion.

The company became a target of the Federal Trade Commission in 2016 after three senators asked for an investigation into how companies like Airbnb affect soaring housing costs. And in October of the same year, Governor Andrew M. Cuomo of New York signed a bill imposing steep fines on Airbnb hosts who break local housing rules.

According to *The New York Times*, both actions were partly the result of the hotel association's plan to suppress Airbnb. "Airbnb is operating a lodging industry, but it is not playing by the same rules," said Troy Flanagan, the American Hotel and Lodging Association's vice president for state and local government affairs, to the newspaper. The association sought to highlight how Airbnb hosts did not collect hotel taxes and were not subject to the same security and safety regulations that hotel operators were required to follow. The association charged that Airbnb hosts ignored rules imposed on hotels including safety and fire inspection standards and anti-discrimination legislation. In some markets, the association said, Airbnb encouraged officials not to collect taxes from Airbnb hosts so as not to legitimize short-term rentals. The industry also forged alliances with hotel labor unions—which it typically opposed on most issues—about how to confront Airbnb.

As *Vox* reported, one analysis found that in the top 25 markets almost a third of Airbnb revenues were generated not by private homeowners and college kids with a room to spare but by commercial listings, defined as whole units rented out more than 180 days per year.

Hotel operators pounced on this, because most large cities strictly regulate short-term commercial rentals. For example, in New York City, Airbnb faced particularly intense government scrutiny, forcing the company to remove thousands of listings from hosts offering not just one but multiple units at once.

In February 2017, Airbnb was sued by Apartment Investment & Management Company (Aimco), which owns or manages about 50,000 properties. The lawsuit charged that Airbnb was deliberately incentivizing people to breach their leases, *The Wall Street Journal* reported.

If this sounds a lot like Uber versus the established taxi and black car industries, you'd be right. And for that reason you might be forgiven for believing that Airbnb somehow represents an evolved model of capitalism and a new, more democratic version of the traditional corporation. The opposite is true.

In this book I've discussed at length the level of *secrecy* provided by conventional accounting methods. When ledgers are private—whether in the hands of the Catholic Church or Enron—the result is opacity and an erosion of trust. And while Airbnb may seem like a groovy new counterculture organization, there's increasing evidence that as far as its finances are concerned, the same old rules apply.

While Airbnb has changed the *marketplace* and how short-term lodgings are bought and sold, its traditional corporate model would make J.P. Morgan envious. The company's revenues, which are considerable, flow directly into the hands of a small number of individual co-founders, private equity partners (the actor Ashton Kutcher is an investor in Airbnb), and institutions including Fidelity Investments and China Broadband Capital.

It may be a new bottle, but inside it's the same old wine. By the way, I am a fan of both Uber and Airbnb, and I use Uber extensively. I am pointing out that while the processes of both companies are somewhat new, the way they cooperate, control, coordinate value, show transparency, and prioritize trust are old, and are not that different from the tricks of the East India Trading Company.

The American Red Cross

Okay, you say, underneath their trendy exteriors, companies like Uber and Airbnb are corporations organized to produce a profit. They may seem innovative in how they interact with the market, but they're still designed to make money for their investors. Surely charitable organizations, which can't declare a profit, are operated with more transparency.

Right?

Not exactly. Big non-profits often operate just like corporations, with a surprising lack of transparency.

Founded in 1881 by Clara Barton, a nurse and teacher, The American Red Cross (ARC) is a humanitarian organization that provides disaster relief, emergency assistance, and education in the United States. Today, the ARC is a nationwide network of more than 650 chapters staffed by 30,000 employees and 500,000 volunteers. In 2014 the organization had $2.9 billion in total revenues.

The ARC has long enjoyed a positive reputation. In 1996, the *Chronicle of Philanthropy*, an industry magazine, published the results of its survey of the popularity and credibility of charitable and non-profit organizations. Of over one hundred charities researched, the survey placed the ARC as the third "most popular charity/non-profit in America."

But transparency is not always a hallmark of the charity's activities.

In June 2016, Laura Sullivan reported for NPR that the ARC's response to the 2010 earthquake in Haiti was marred by sloppy accounting and unchecked spending. The report followed a lengthy investigation by US Senator Chuck Grassley and his staff, spurred by coverage of the Red Cross's Haiti response by NPR and ProPublica. In the wake of the disaster the ARC raised nearly $500 million, more than any other nonprofit, and announced an ambitious plan to build housing for earthquake victims The main focus of the project—called LAMIKA, an acronym in Creole for "A

Better Life in My Neighborhood"—was to construct hundreds of permanent homes. Reports indicate that years after the earthquake ravaged the island, the ARC and LAMIKA had built just six permanent homes.

Senator Grassley's investigators found the ARC spent a quarter of the donated cash — or almost $125 million — on its own internal expenses, far more than the charity previously had disclosed. The report also charged the charity's top executives blocked congressional investigators and that financial information about its Haiti program was incomplete. The report charged that ARC told congressional investigators that $70 million spent on "program expenses" included funds to oversee and evaluate its Haiti programs. But Grassley's office found that the charity "is unable to provide any financial evidence that oversight activities in fact occurred."

As Justin Elliott and Laura Sullivan wrote for ProPubica, "The Red Cross won't disclose details of how it has spent the hundreds of millions of dollars donated for Haiti. But our reporting shows that less money reached those in need than the Red Cross has said."

Trust gap? Not according to the American Red Cross.

Can the venerable charity police itself? Apparently not; the Grassley Report stated the ARC has kept the organization's own ethics unit and internal investigations "severely undermanned and underfunded," and the charity "appears to be reluctant to support the very unit that is designed to police wrongdoing within the organization."

The Grassley Report concluded, "There are substantial and fundamental concerns about [the Red Cross] as an organization."

Opportunity 8: Break Out Of Opaqueness

How's that for new or trusted corporate models? The reality of commerce today is that we transact in a trust gap, and regardless of the model or the archetype of the corporation, commerce is being strained by an increasing need to be re-platformed. Not even the so-called new commercial models are any new.

9. Enter the Blockchain Protocol

We've seen that in regard to how humans organize themselves into value-creating organizations, during the past few
centuries little has changed.

It was thousands of years ago when merchants and rulers
first began keeping records of account, inked onto papyrus
or chiseled onto a piece of stone.

In the fourteenth century, double entry bookkeeping
emerged.

In 1602, the Dutch East India Company was chartered as
the first modern stock corporation.

Since then, despite the dazzling progress of technology, the
corporation remains the same. While *ownership* can be
spread out among many people—today the company with
the most outstanding shares of stock is ExxonMobil, with
5.4 million shares held by investors—*control* remains con-
centrated among the few who have access the company's
full set of accounts. Ledgers can be hidden, different versions made for different audiences, and money shifted
around in accounts like a game of three-card monte.

In terms of transparency and trust, the corporation of today is no different than it was a century ago.

But a paradigm shift is at hand.

If we think about the paradigm shifts leading the to Ages of Kingdoms, Commerce, Mercantilism and Colonialism, Industry, and Information, we can argue that we are about to enter the Institutional Revolution, which will change the way we organize and govern ourselves. With each of the previous paradigms there are attributes of commerce that trended in a consistent direction. For example, we can argue that the quality of life of our species in the aggregate gets better with each paradigm, the cost per transaction continues to get lower with each paradigm, and the speed of commerce continues to increase with each paradigm. In addition, with each paradigm the distribution of wealth continues to flatten (of course, not enough as yet).

Let's look at a few large paradigms that have transformed human society because they changed something fundamentally important forever. Every paradigm came at a moment in history when humanity was confronted with a *gap* that needed to be bridged.

The Knowledge Gap

Around the year 1450, the advent of Gutenberg's printing press filled a massive *knowledge gap*. Prior to the invention of movable type and the printing press, academic knowledge—in Europe, chiefly in the form of the Bible and classical texts—was the exclusive province of the privileged few. Books were written and copied by hand. To produce just one

Bible took thousands of hours of labor. The resulting object was highly valued and retained by a prince or priest, who interpreted its contents for the masses from the pulpit. Few Christian believers had actually *read* the Bible; they were *told* what it said by those who had access to one. The mass-produced Bible made it possible for ordinary believers to read it for themselves, and to make up their own minds about its meaning.

The printing press introduced a standard of uniformity of language in printed materials. Prior to the printing press, words were individually scribed according to the local custom, with idiosyncratic writing, grammar, and handwriting. The printing press, which made multiple identical copies, brought about a new consistency in spelling, grammar and punctuation. By virtue of the increased uniformity and reliability of the written work—*trust*, if you will—readers were able to consistently receive the thoughts and ideas of writers.

With the invention of the printing press and the manufacture of identical books of at an economical price and with high quality, books were now more available and affordable to the general public. In prior centuries, the average person had little incentive to learn how to read, any more than the average person of today has an incentive to learn how to fly an airplane. Reading and writing just weren't things you needed to do. Over the decades, as more information through the written word was accessible and disseminated, levels of literacy rose throughout Europe, and with it came increased consensus.

The printing press strengthened the sciences and rational inquiry. Natural philosophers—scientists as we call them today—were more readily able to share and exchange information. Diagrams and illustrations, which in the past were individually hand drawn, could be reproduced in quantity. This produced a reciprocating effect, as the new ability to reproduce diagrams, pictures, and tables for peer consumption encouraged scholars to produce accurate and useful illustrations. The dissemination of scientific knowledge through the use of manufactured books and documents further increased literacy as more individuals gained access to emerging knowledge and made it available for the next person to continue or build on previous research.

By the end of the fifteenth century printing shops were proliferating throughout Europe, with an estimated three hundred in Germany alone. The business of printing and selling of books exploded. The Harry Ransom Humanities Research Center estimated that before the invention of the printing press, the total number of books in all of Europe was around thirty thousand. By the year 1500, the book was well entrenched as an industrial object, and the number of books in Europe had grown to as many as twelve million copies of teens of thousands of titles.

Gutenberg's invention closed the knowledge gap and gave millions of people access to information in its printed form.

The Power Gap

In the nineteenth century, the steam engine filled the *power gap*. For thousands of years, to perform work, human beings had three sources of power: their own muscles, domesticated draft animals, and natural sources (wind and water).

These were each very limited, both in the amount of power they could provide and in their reliability. Farmers were limited by how much an ox or horse could plow. Mills were limited by the amount of water rushing through a spillway. Ships were limited by the direction and force of the wind. Humans, like blacksmiths, were limited by the endurance and strength of their muscles.

As the human population grew, requiring more food and more goods, the power gap became critically burdensome. In 1781, Scottish inventor James Watt developed an engine powered by the force of expanding steam, whose kinetic energy was transformed into the continuous rotary motion of an axle. Watt's engines soon enabled a wide range of manufacturing machinery, ships, and eventually railroad cars to be independently powered. A significant advantage was that steam engines could be sited anywhere that water and fuel—coal or wood—could be obtained. Even better, unlike a draft animal, when you weren't using the engine you could just turn it off and let it sit there—you didn't have to constantly feed it! The steam engine became the driving force of the Industrial Revolution, allowing factories to be constructed virtually anywhere. As they grew in size, steam engines became capable of producing vast amounts of power that humans had once only dreamed of. In the early twentieth century the steam engine was supplanted by the even more powerful and portable internal combustion engine, making possible powered flight.

The steam engine—and later the internal combustion engine—closed the power gap and allowed human beings to massively increase their industrial productivity.

The Distance Gap

The Internet—as well as the broad emergence of digital technology—closed the *distance gap*. If you're under the age of thirty, it may be hard to believe that prior to the mid-1990s, when the Internet emerged as a potent tool for communication, the fax machine was the state-of-the-art method for transmitting information quickly across long distances. Fax machines operated over telephone landlines. They transmitted scanned printed material to a telephone number connected to a printer or other output device. The original document was scanned and processed into a bitmap, and then transmitted through phone lines in the form of audio-frequency tones. The receiving fax machine received the tones and reconstructed the image, printing a paper copy.

At the time, it was amazing technology.

This was a time when on every street corner was a pay phone, and you had to keep pumping quarters into it when the recorded voice told you your three minutes were up.

And if you wanted to go shoe shopping, unless you ordered from a mail-order catalogue, which could take weeks for delivery, you had to get in your car and drive to a shoe store. See a movie? You had to go to a movie theatre. The Internet brought all of these things, and more, to your home computer and eventually your smart phone. From your office in Puerto Rico, would you like to read this morning's issue of the *South China Morning Post*? No need to fly to Hong Kong—you can read it on your phone. Do you want to see today's political demonstrations in Paris or Cairo? Just go to YouTube and you'll get a street-level view.

Each of these paradigms changed something fundamental for almost every member of the human species, and the changes these paradigms have created for humanity are permanent. They are forever.

Paradigm shifts both large and small are triggered by something big. The abolition of forced labor was a trigger, the Industrial Age was a trigger, and the Internet was a trigger.

Blockchain will be a trigger for the Institutional Revolution.

What will blockchain change forever? It will change something that is extremely fundamental to every human being, and how every human being interacts with the individuals and organizations around them. It will change something that, looking back at each paradigm change—the printing press, the steam engine, the Internet—has not yet been affected.

This is *trust*.

The Growing Trust Gap

Throughout history, as paradigms shifted the problem of trust remained. As we have seen in this book thus far, from the days of clay tablets and papyrus rolls our standards of interpersonal and business trust haven't changed. People still cheat each other the same way they've been cheating each other for centuries. And with the Internet, the stakes have only gotten higher. Those expensive new shoes you wanted to buy? In 1990, you went to the shoe store and inspected them. You could talk to the shoe salesperson. You knew where to go if you had a problem with them. Today, you order shoes from a website. You do not interact with humans. You don't know where your shoes come from—they just appear at your door. Your level of trust with the online shoe store needs to be very high, but the Internet tends to work in the other direction by eroding trust.

As Mary Anne Patton and Audun Jøsang wrote in their 2004 report "Technologies for Trust in Electronic Commerce," published by Queensland University of Technology, "Most traditional cues for assessing trust in the physical world are not available online.... Consumers perceive the Web as a world of chaos, offering both opportunities and threats. Factors affecting trust in e-commerce for consumers include security risks, privacy issues, and lack of reliability in e-commerce processes in general."

They reported that consumers typically have no opportunity to inspect and touch products offered online, or to fully evaluate a service before making a purchase decision. Information about the physical location of a merchant or the source of the product is often vague or absent.

When compared with traditional commerce, ecommerce is more automated, more impersonal, entails more legal uncertainties, provides little sensory information about the products, and presents more opportunities for fraud and abuse.

A lack of trust can impede the growth of commerce. In a May 2016 post, the National Telecommunications & Information Administration (NTIA), part of the U.S. Department of Commerce, said that if consumers have concerns about security and privacy, economic activity on the Internet may not be as robust as it could be. "Every day, billions of people around the world use the Internet to share ideas, conduct financial transactions, and keep in touch with family, friends, and colleagues," Rafi Goldberg, policy analyst, Office of Policy Analysis and Development at NTIA, wrote in the post. "Users send and store personal medical data, business communications, and even intimate conversations over this global network. But for the Internet to grow and thrive, users must continue to trust that their personal information will be secure and their privacy protected."

The problem is more acute in developing nations. As Helen Leggatt wrote in 2011 in "Lack of trust in online payments curbs ecommerce in Middle East," a report released by Dubai-based market research firm Real Opinions revealed that in the Middle East only six percent of Internet users regularly shop online. The reason for the low numbers? Consumers don't trust online payment systems.

As Leggatt wrote, "Nearly half (43%) of Internet users in the Middle East have been put off buying products online because they don't trust online payment systems. Not even the launches of big daily deal sites in the region, such as Groupon or its local and more popular competitor Cobone, have swayed consumers to part with their money online."

In July 2016, *The Paypers* reported that "Consumers in Thailand report lack of trust in ecommerce security" and the Thai Commerce & Payment Study conducted with DataOne Asia showed that 32% of respondents had experienced personal payment fraud within the last twelve months. ATMs, ecommerce, and mobile commerce were the three primary sources of fraud. Few consumers in Thailand believe their payment credentials are protected from fraud when using m-commerce and ecommerce.

Online identity is also in crisis.

Online daters are all too familiar with fake profiles and misleading photos. What about Tinder on a blockchain? We all know friends or family members—our perhaps even ourselves—who have had the unpleasant experience of meeting the person whose profile we found attractive only to find the person was very different. On their online profile they lied about their age, their weight, the fact that they didn't have a job... the list of such transgressions is long. You probably chuckled about Tinder on a blockchain, how about LinkedIn on a blockchain?

Some of the big dating sites are beginning to address the problem of people who lie about themselves. To create more transparency about age and real first names, location-based dating apps like Tinder and The Grade are forcing their members to connect through Facebook, which has at least *some* controls over misrepresentation. Yes the state of the fidelity of digital identity is in such crisis, that connecting through Facebook is the state of the art! The Grade also asks users to rank their dates on a scale from A+ to F based on three criteria: quality of messages, profile photos and description, and peer review. As the website says, "With The Grade, we hold users accountable for their behavior with our unique algorithm. The Grade expels users permanently who get an 'F' grade!"

The trust gap doesn't only exist online. In today's global economy, we routinely buy products that may have come to us from halfway around the world. What do we really know about these products?

For example, I happen to like tangerines. I think they taste good, and they're good for you. However, I'm allergic to the pesticides and other chemicals that growers commonly apply to their tangerines. For this reason I buy organic tangerines.

You know where this is going.

How do you know that the food item you're buying at the grocery store is truly organic?

Is it because the store displays the item in a bin with a big sign saying, "Organic produce"? And on each piece of fruit there's a little sticker that says, "Certified organic"?

Do you trust these assertions? Maybe. Maybe not.

In the United States, tangerines are grown on farms in Arizona, California, Florida, and Texas. If you buy a tangerine at a store in New York City, that tangerine has been through a long supply chain, from orchard to distributor to warehouse to the supermarket.

Organic tangerines need to be grown in certified organic orchards, which use no chemicals or growth hormones. Instead of chemical fertilizers, organic growers use natural compost and manure to encourage growth. They never use chemical herbicides or fungicides. And instead of chemical pesticides to control pests and disease, they rely on beneficial birds and insects.

Proof of organic certification is often conveyed by a green and white USDA Organic sticker, meaning the tangerines have met the strict standards overseeing the growth, harvesting, and handling of the fruit. But these organic stickers are voluntary, and other labels, such as "naturally grown," don't mean "organic" and are pointless because they have no set of regulations to meet.

How do I know the tangerine I buy at the store is organic? I have no choice but to trust the merchant. For all I know, there could be a guy in the back room slapping a little "organic" sticker on every piece of chemical-soaked fruit coming through the back door.

Blockchain Closes the Trust Gap

How can blockchain close the trust gap between the grocer and me? It's simple: At the time of harvesting, the farmer puts a quick response (QR) code sticker on the fruit. In the store, I can scan the QR code with my phone and be taken to the fruit company's data center where a blockchain will provide a complete history of the farm and the fruit: The method of fertilization, insect control, date of harvest, shipping route—everything I need to be assured that what I'm paying for is actually what I'm getting.

Another trust gap closed!

As the trigger, for the first time in centuries blockchain stands to improve the level of trust in transactions. The movement of trust to a level of virtual abundance will have exponential effects on the attributes of commerce that have been trending prior, such as cost per transaction.

Blockchain will change how people trust us, how we trust each other, and how organizations are trusted.

We will simply trust differently.

From the invention of blockchain onwards, we will abundantly trust data, information, organizations, governments and each other differently. This change in how we trust will change the experience of being a human being forever. We are currently focusing on adding financial and accounting data to blockchains, but eventually we will add other data sets such as identity data, reputation data, inventory data, market data, agreement data, cooperate data, and others data sets. All of these data sets will go through the blockchain maturity model of first being trusted, then used to drive easy consensus, and eventually good candidates forming the bedrock for autonomous actions.

How about the corporate structure? Consider that today we only have the same familiar corporate structures (S-Corp, C-Corp, etc.) to choose from. These are known templates of corporations that we use to lead, manage, govern, and report. If you are I were to form a corporate structure that does not fit any of these known templates, we would not be recognized because it would not be trusted or transparent. In the future, I expect us to be able to load up new corporate structures into a blockchain that is immutable and transparent. These new corporate structures will be more likely to be recognized as legitimate because their "rules" are loaded into a blockchain. This is where consensus around decisions and spending in these new structures become very transparent, and trusted.

This will then give rise to the distributed autonomous organization (DAO), which I'll discuss in more in the pages ahead.

But we're getting too far ahead of ourselves. Our first ask is to properly introduce the blockchain protocol and then see how it's a true transformation in how we introduce a new and profound level of trust, and subsequently re-organize the creation and distribution of value via this Institutional Revolution.

A Simplified Introduction to Blockchain

The blockchain protocol was created in 2008 by a person or group of people known by the pseudonym Satoshi Nakamoto. This is the name used by the unknown person or persons who designed bitcoin, which we'll discuss later, and created its original reference implementation, including the first blockchain database.

Who is Nakamoto? No one knows. He has claimed to be a man living in Japan, born on April 5, 1975. However, speculation about the true identity of Nakamoto has mostly focused on a number of cryptography and computer science experts of non-Asian descent, living in the United States and Europe. An Australian programmer named Craig Steven Wright has claimed to be Nakamoto, though he has not yet offered proof of this.

Enough about Nakamoto. Entire books could be written about his or her presumed identity. The thing we want talk about is blockchain.

The blockchain protocol has two fundamental features that distinguish it from any other method of recording and disseminating information.

1. Authority Is Distributed Into The Network

The simplest image of blockchain is that of an expandable spreadsheet duplicated across any number of computers, from two to millions. Then imagine that this spreadsheet instantly updates whenever an individual operator makes a change.

Information held on a blockchain exists as a shared, and continually reconciled, database. The blockchain database isn't "owned" by any single operator, meaning the records it keeps are truly communal. No centralized version of this information exists for a hacker to corrupt. Hosted by millions of computers simultaneously if on a public blockchain (hundreds if on a private blockchain), its data is accessible to anyone with the appropriate permissions and the ability to demonstrate that said access would be used for an approved intent.

Imagine a mainframe computer in 1970. Chances are, the "network" (if you can call it that) by which the massive mainframe computer was accessed resembled a wheel with spokes. At the hub of the wheel stood the mainframe computer. The spokes were the individual terminals through which the human operators interacted with the computer. The terminals didn't talk to each other, only to the mainframe. A ledger held by the mainframe was no different than a ledger kept by the head monk in a medieval abbey: if you wanted to see it, you had to ask permission. It was a *centralized* system.

Next, imagine a typical network with computers linked together. This *decentralized* system resembles a suburban cul-de-sac, with a cluster of houses connected to a street, which then links that cluster to another cluster, and to another cluster. From one house you can access any other house in the subdivision, but not directly—you have to go out into the street and then go into the driveway of the house you're visiting. You cannot go directly from your house to any other house. You have to go via the street. If you have a ledger in your house, it's easy to keep it hidden, because access to your house is limited.

Now imagine if every house were *directly linked* to every other house in the subdivision. Therefore, from any given house you could communicate directly with any other house. You would not need to go out into the street. In this *distributed ledger* system, you couldn't "hide" your ledger because the ledger would only exist as a *shared artifact*. There would be no "original" ledger. No one household could claim special rights to it because there would be no master copy, only dozens of identical copies throughout the system. Access again, driven by permission and used only for approved intent.

But how could this shared ledger be updated with new entries?

Very simply. If you made a change in your copy of the ledger, that change would instantly appear in the ledgers of all the other houses, along with information identifying the time and place the change was made. So if in the distributed ledger you entered, "On Saturday afternoon, the Smith household had a yard sale and sold $200.00 worth of stuff from our attic," everyone else's ledger would instantly reflect that same information.

Like the Internet as compared to a company intranet, blockchains can be public or private. The differences relate to the default permissions built into the network to allow new blocks to be written to the chain. Public blockchains have proof of work (work for which is paid for with bitcoins or some other digital currency). Before it is written to the system, each transaction is verified and synced with every node affiliated with the blockchain. Until this has occurred, the next transaction cannot move forward.

Private blockchains, such as a smaller network of known or ancillary parties (an industry chain so to speak) will have *proof of stake*. In a private chain, the permissions for block creation are restricted and control over the chain is given to specific trusted entities.

2. Data Is Immutable

The democratic, decentralized qualities of blockchain databases are only half the story. The other half is that unlike typical Excel spreadsheets, each new entry—or updated version of the file—is mathematically "chained" to the previous one, and so on, all the way back to the original. Thus, over time one blockchain file could consist of hundreds or thousands of evolving versions. It's like the rings of a tree: Each ring is an immutable record of the tree's growth during one year. Once a ring is grown by the tree, it cannot be altered.

With a regular spreadsheet or document, if someone makes an alteration and then saves the new version by giving it a new name, the new file exists wholly independently from the previous version. It *replaces* the previous version, which can then be deleted as if it never existed. You can have version

#50 of a document, with the first forty-nine versions gone forever, or, in a cumbersome protocol, saved to an archive somewhere.

This immutability adds yet another element of trust. It's what makes the bitcoin monetary system possible, which I'll touch upon in the pages ahead. It also makes fraud much more difficult, because every change to a file is recorded forever. You can't "wipe it clean."

We've seen how the problem of trust has persisted through many centuries and many paradigm shifts. As the years rolled past, the trust gap stayed wide—or even got wider—in commerce, online dating, the food we eat, and many other areas of human activity. Let's now turn our attention to a real-world subject that has occupied much of this book—the problem with corporate ledgers and how they've been easily manipulated by the people who control the corporate purse strings.

Looking back at the history of the ledger, the problem of trust keeps rearing its ugly head.

Could investors trust the ledgers of the Dutch East India Company?

Or Sunbeam? Enron? Walmart? How about private companies like Uber and Airbnb, or the Vatican Bank? Or big non-profits like the American Red Cross?

No matter how far back you go in history, whenever you combine wealth with limited access to information, you eventually get fraud. This is because ledgers can be *hidden* and they can be *falsified.*

In a ledger, you store information by adding or deleting one row at a time to or from a database. Some electronic spreadsheets are outdated and don't have a change log built in, so if you start with ten records, and delete one, there is really no change log to reflect that one record was deleted, and no easy way to investigate if the database was tampered with.

Ledgers with change logs attached to them will write change entries into another database storing that something was "added" or "removed," or there were "debits" and/or "credits." These ledgers with change logs make it less difficult to spot when data was tampered with. But as easily as someone can tamper with the data, they can also add or delete the entries in the change log, again making it difficult to spot when data was tampered with.

Ledgers today are not always trusted, and as a consequence we have to verify them with some form of an intermediary who can provide verification. These third-party verifiers are independent auditors and government agencies, who we know from past experience can be either lazy or themselves corrupt. These intermediaries manufacture trust needed to power global commerce, but too often they fall flat and trust is destroyed.

3. Security Is Managed By Keys and Signatures

In simplified form, here is how a blockchain distributed ledger works, as opposed to our current centralized ledgers.

In a distributed ledger, each initial record is assigned a unique key that relates to the person or party who makes the entry. Each subsequent record that is written to the ledger is assigned another unique key. The unique key for the subsequent record is calculated by a formula that takes as its input the entire contents of all previous records and then crunches it in a "key calculating formula" to create a new derived key.

Therefore record two has a unique key that was derived from all of the data in record one, including the key to record one, and record three has a unique key that was derived from the combination of all of the data and key in record two and record one, and so on and so on.

As you can see, each new record is chained to all of the records that existed before it. As a result one can now use an algorithm to check for tampering of a ledger by looking at the entire ledger as an aggregate, and detect alterations because any record that was removed or altered will be easy to spot because it will break the chain.

This application of encryption keys and algorithms creates an immutable record of information for storing data sets such as finance data, identity data, reputation data, inventory data, market data, agreement data, cooperate data, and others data sets—for individuals and for organizations.

This type of immutable ledger removes a large amount of the rationale for verification by intermediaries, and significantly increases the trust in data, because it is less likely that the data can be tampered with. Or at a minimum it will be exponentially simpler and less expensive to tell if data was tampered with or not.

This is only one of several parts of blockchain, but the value is clear.

There are other parts, such as having these immutable ledgers stored on a network of multiple computers, and at pre-defined blocks or intervals algorithms check each copy of the distributed ledger on all nodes of the network, to make sure that no one ledger has been tampered with; comparing all of the copies of ledgers of the network together leads to consensus and proof of authenticity.

If we just focus on the increase of trust of a blockchain distributed ledger compared to the low trust of a traditional ledger, the result is that the increase of trust in information representing finance data, identity data, reputation data, inventory data, market data, agreement data, cooperate data, and other data sets significantly lowers the need for intermediaries.

Companies that will use immutable distributed ledgers instead of tamper-able traditional ledgers, and leverage the rest of blockchain will operate with high levels of trust requiring low levels of intermediaries.

We live, and we transact, but we operate on the assumption that counterparties cannot be trusted, because let's face it they can't, really; and we carry the burden of this trust vacuum by having to verify almost every aspect of our lives. We live in a world of fake identities, misleading reputations, and unreliable inventory and ownership. To protect ourselves we are forced to use expensive, cumbersome, and time consuming intermediaries to verify data for us. It's like the complicated Ptolemaic solar system—you can argue that the math works, but it's an unwieldy and overly complex solution, especially when a simpler and more powerful solution is at our fingertips.

Imagine if at Enron the company's ledgers, which were obfuscated and made grotesquely complex to shield malfeasance, had instead been based on a blockchain protocol, and the permitted parties with the appropriate permission and intent included the board of directors, the independent auditors, and a government oversight agency such as the Securities and Exchange Commission. The successful commission of fraud would have required a vast number of co-conspirators including government regulators. It's nearly inconceivable that someone wouldn't have blown the whistle at the first sign of impropriety, and the losses would have been minimal.

This new paradigm of blockchain will forever change the way we look at trust between parties, and because of the burden associated with manufacturing trust, emerging "trust companies" built on blockchains that take advantage not only of distributed ledgers but "smart" contracts are going to supplant current untrusted companies.

Smart contracts are emerging because distributed ledgers enable the coding of contracts programmed to execute when consensus is met on specified conditions supported by trusted data.

At the technology's current level of development, smart contracts can be programmed to perform simple functions. For example, in a smart contract, an asset or currency is transferred into a program. At a mutually agreed upon point, the program validates a condition via consensus and selects to whom the asset should be delivered, or a refund issued to the person who sent it. Meanwhile, the decentralized ledger also stores and replicates the document, giving it security and immutability.

A Word About Bitcoin

Anytime you talk about blockchain, people want to know about bitcoin, because it's well known and the concept is intriguing. I like to say that bitcoin is to blockchain what AOL Chat was to the Internet—it's interesting, but it's not at the center of this discussion.

Nevertheless, it needs to be touched upon.

Bitcoin is a cryptocurrency and an electronic payment system invented by the mysterious Satoshi Nakamoto. Introduced on October 31, 2008 to a cryptography mailing list, bitcoin was released as open-source software in 2009. The system is peer-to-peer, and transactions to exchange a digital currency take place between users directly, without an intermediary. These transactions are verified by network nodes and recorded in the blockchain. This is mostly a public blockchain.

To vastly oversimplify, each bitcoin user has an account. If John wants to send Mary a payment in bitcoin, he simply sends it to her account, along with a digital signature to ensure authenticity.

So far, this is roughly analogous to any other mobile money transfer system.

There are two key differences. One difference is the bitcoin authentication system is more complicated. In the bitcoin system, John must use his *private* electronic "key." He sends his money not to Mary directly, but to her *public* key. It's like her bank account number. To claim her money, Mary must use her private key, which is like her bank account password, to verify she's the recipient. (If you lose your private key, you lose access to your bitcoin. There's no bank or government agency to which you can appeal!) You may remember the hawala discussed earlier, Bitcoin is a trust and transparency upgrade of the hawala at epic scale and global scope.

Each time John sends money, the system creates a new and unique mathematical signature for John. This signature is not his private key; instead, it proves that the sender is indeed John. To eliminate theft, the signature is never the same twice—it's generated anew with each transaction.

The second difference is in how the records of the transaction are kept.

In a bank-based money transfer, the account book—the ledger—is kept by the bank. When John sends Mary ten dollars from his mobile money account, his bank, which holds his funds, acts as the record keeper. This is the way it's been done for centuries.

In a bitcoin transaction, there is no bank and no bank balance. Instead, there's a distributed ledger that's held by "maintainers" across the globe. When John sends Mary a bitcoin payment, the notification of that transaction is sent to all the maintainers so that it appears in every instance of the distributed ledger. Maintainers are the "miners" that work to maintain the operation and sanctity of a public blockchain. Miners are compensated with the digital currency of the blockchain they maintain, in the case of the public Bitcoin blockchain, miners are compensated for their chain maintenance with Bitcoin.

In the event of an error or corruption entering an individual ledger, there's a consensus system whereby the majority of ledger keepers can overwrite the tiny minority who show a different transaction.

The integrity of bitcoin is based on the assumption that creating a fraud embraced by the majority of maintainers would be extremely expensive and impractical.

Also, there's no "bank balance" in the traditional sense. John just can't simply glance at one number and see how much he's got. Instead, his available funds are verified by the historical records of his "inputs"—that is, the bitcoin deposits that have been made into his account. If he sends Mary five bitcoin, these five bitcoin must match a total of five bitcoin that he has received. It's like depositing a five-dollar bill into your bank account, and then, as identified by its unique serial number, using that *same exact five-dollar bill* to pay Mary. In a sense, bitcoin tracks the journey of that unique five-dollar bill as it goes from person to person. The record of its journey is complete and immutable.

But, you say, this is a virtual monetary system that's maintained by the last people on earth you should trust: *strangers on the Internet!* Why on earth would anyone want to entrust their money to a bunch of random people all over the world?

The beauty of bitcoin—and of blockchain—is that trust in particular individuals is not necessary. Your trust is not in this or that person, whom you never know; your trust is in the bitcoin system and the community as a whole as they prove themselves to you over multiple transactions.

Trust in bitcoin is growing. According to a study published by Cambridge University in 2017, there are between 2.9 million and 5.8 million unique users actively using a cryptocurrency wallet, with most of them using bitcoin. This represents a sharp increase from 2013, when the number of active users was estimated to be between 0.3 to 1.3 million.

Bitcoin can be exchanged for dollars. As of this writing, the value of one bitcoin, which since its launch in 2008 has gone up and down, was up. In January 2017, Larry Light at CBS Moneywatch noted that the value of bitcoin had topped $1,000 for the first time since 2013. The research firm Coindesk had pegged bitcoin's price at a peak of $1,125 in late 2013, then sharply down to a low of $210 in January 2015. Driving the surge in 2016 and 2017 was a flood of buyers in India and China, where government crackdowns on moving money abroad resulted in increased adoption of bitcoin and other cryptocurrencies. Light reported that as of January 2017 the worldwide value of bitcoin was $16.4 billion.

To be sure, bitcoin remains controversial. To its supporters, it's an efficient means of money transfer that's non-inflationary and anonymous, and beyond the long reach of government authority over the currency supply. To its critics, it's basically a conduit for illegal activity and a scheme that can cost people money.

But one thing is certain: the blockchain protocol, of which bitcoin is a small part, has the potential to usher in a paradigm shift of what I call abundant trust, and with it the Institutional Revolution that will rival the Digital Revolution and Industrial Revolution before it.

10. From Abundant Trust to Consensus

We've traced the emergence and history of the blockchain protocol, and how the combination of many existing and tested inventions created a distributed ledger, and the resulting blossoming of trust in abundance. We are entering a world of commerce where trust is inherent, instead of having to be manufactured. With blockchain, trust is established not by powerful intermediaries like governments, banks, and technology companies, but through community collaboration and well written code. The distributed ledger creates a condition where trust can germinate among hundreds of microscopic movements as well as the few large ones that everyone knows and reports on. It's that "ambient tidal wave" that creates the revolution, not just the ability to avoid the few well-known catastrophes.

Looking ahead, many categories of data will go through the "trust machine." The first are accounting and financial data, which have been the focus of this book. Eventually, more data sets will move to the blockchain fabric, creating new waves of marketplace re-shaping. I believe other categories will follow. They are:

1. **Finance** – This is where we are today, with bitcoin and distributed financial ledgers.

2. **Identity** – Where we go next.

3. **Reputation** – This follows identity.

4. **Inventory** – Has implications on ownership and rights, and ownership fragmentation.

5. **Market** – What I offer in exchange for value, non-currency value. Commons markets and catallaxy market, which I'll discuss in the pages ahead. (Catallaxy was made popular by Friedrich Hayek, who defined it as "the order brought about by the mutual adjustment of many individual economies in a market." It refers to a marketplace of ideas, where people holding diverse political ideologies come together to gain deeper understanding of a wide range of political orientations.) Maybe my next writing will be on identifying early demand signals in a supply chains, predicative markets, heterogeneous currencies, and instant liquidity of anything (physical or virtual) of value. I am going to need more ink!

6. **Agreement** – Why we exist, how we operate, and how we manage unexpected circumstances—a world free of conflict.

7. **Cooperate** - How we organize into a corporative to create and capture value, and how we govern the operations of said corporative.

With trust comes easier consensus and more autonomous markets.

Beyond Lowering Transaction Costs

Much of the excitement around the blockchain protocol has centered around its potential to revolutionize the financial services industry by reducing the cost and risk of financial transactions, improving transparency, and bringing financial services to billions of people who can't afford traditional banks. But its influence will soon go far beyond as the blockchain protocol significantly lowers many transaction costs. A global searchable database of all transactions would reduce the costs of search. Smart contracts—programs designed to execute a set of instructions when consensus around certain conditions are met—on the blockchain protocol will cut the expense of making contracts, enforcing them, and making payments. Autonomous agents, which are bundles of smart contracts on the blockchain, pave the way to lower agency and coordinating costs, and may foreshadow highly distributed enterprises with minimal management.

Take Uber, for example. Earlier in this book I discussed Uber—not to pick on them, for there are plenty of other examples—and while the company may have the outward appearance of a groovy "community" company, it's really just an old-fashioned private corporation that funnels its profits to the few equity holders. But the blockchain protocol could facilitate the creation of a truly trust-abundant and consensus-based corporative. Blockchain's distributed ledgers could allow passengers and drivers, who are strangers to each other and have no particular reason to trust each other, to securely exchange information through decentralized networks, without the cost of intermediaries. This can reduce both costs and time for every participant.

Every driver's application and registration would include any criminal record, his or her driving record, proof of vehicle ownership and registration, and evidence of insurance and safety inspections you can trust without intermediaries because it would be easy to see if the underlying data on a blockchain was tampered with. Smart contracts would maintain a round-the-clock vigil for timely insurance, permit, and inspection renewals. By creating a blockchain cooperative for taxis, the drivers will receive all the wealth they create.

With consensus comes the notion that we can agree on the value of something without having to represent that value in terms of its equivalent in currency. For example, what is the value of a hug, or a high five? Like in a barter system, could a hug be exchanged for some measurement of enhanced reputation?

Until the blockchain protocol, for every transaction (the fulfillment of an order, where a good or service is exchange for "payment"), on the other side of the transaction was also some fiat currency. The blockchain, with its ability to record every detail of transactions that are trusted, can introduce the ability to describe value in things other than currency. This is where we see "commons" markets where value is not always currency and markets can run on heterogeneous currencies and token types, vs. catallaxy markets, where currency is key.

The other side of the transaction, without intermediaries, can be non-currency. Yes, bitcoin tokens can help here, but we are looking at a new value system—one that takes us back to bartering, in low-cost highly trusted micro-exchanges at global scale with parties that don't know each other.

What do we call this state of the world? Frictionless commerce?

To get back to the idea of consensus emerging from an abundance of trust, I've devised a simple formula that illustrates how we build consensus:

Trust + Community = Consensus

We ask ourselves what is the current state of consensus— is there anything that we agree on? Can we agree on identity? Laws? Rules of morality? These are easy, but can we agree on the price or value of something? Or the rating of a car's safety versus another? Or the efficacy of a medicine?

Here the emergence of consensus gets really interesting!

We can imagine some use cases for private, commercial, and public situations where consensus is in abundance. Again it's important to separate the use cases from what is just basic human rights, what is the opportunity for communities or countries, what is the opportunity for commerce, and what is the opportunity for a broader social collaborative body (such as the UN).

La'Zooz

In Israel, former yoga instructor Shay Zluf co-founded La'Zooz, a cooperative ride-sharing service using the blockchain protocol as a base layer of the technology stack. Through the organization's app, car owners give people rides in exchange for tokens, which in turn they can later trade for rides from other members of the community. As Gabrielle Coppola and Yaacov Benmeleh wrote in their 2015 article published by Bloomberg entitled "This Israeli Ride-Sharing App Is the Utopian, Hippie Uber," the creative team behind La'Zooz, which means "to move" in Hebrew, talks a lot about alleviating city congestion, saving the environment, community responsibility, and the fair share of wealth. "Just doing another application was not enough for me," Zluf, a former contract developer for eBay and Broadcom, told the authors. "What is important for me is to start a movement."

To keep the service fully autonomous, even for payments, in 2013 La'Zooz began developing its own cryptocurrency, "zooz." In addition to being used as a carrier of value to compensate drivers, zooz tokens are awarded to the roughly eighty coders and other people who volunteer services to improve the app. La'Zooz is a loosely knit community: users can book rides using tokens earned by driving others or by contributing to the development of the app and enhancing their own value and reputation to the community

Using the same technology underlying bitcoin, the La'Zooz network exists not on a central server like Uber and Lyft but on the smartphones and computers of its community of users. And instead of bitcoin's proof of work method by which bitcoin "miners" earn new tokens, a process requiring vast computational power, La'Zooz generates new zooz tokens with "proof of movement." You essentially turn on your La'Zooz-enabled smartphone and drive your fares where they want to go. As you drive, you earn zooz tokens, which, when you want a ride from someone else in the La'Zooz community, you can pay from your purse of zooz.

There are other ways to earn zooz tokens, at least initially. As the La'Zooz website said in April 2017, "Early adopters help in establishing the social transportation network in their location and therefore should be rewarded. In this first phase, users can mine Road Zooz tokens by simply installing the app and riding with it in the background sharing valuable traffic pattern data to the community. Road Zooz tokens will be usable within the app to reward drivers for sharing a ride once the service is running.... The La'Zooz community encourages its early users to spread the App to new active users by compensating sharing of the App with zooz tokens. The reward for spreading the App is explained in the Road miners protocol.... The community can decide to encourage certain user behaviors. For example, a user creating a rich profile with personal details, a photo, goals in life, etc. will contribute higher value for the community in many ways. Thus the community can reward rich profiles with zooz tokens."

As of April 2017, the cash value of a zooz was one US cent. But this is essentially a barter system, where value is created and stored outside the universe of everyday currency. As a driver, you trade your work driving a passenger for the reward of then being driven by someone else. The social benefit is that instead of two trips (you and the other person) requiring two uses of an automobile (since each trip is taken alone), the same two trips now require only one use of an automobile, because the car is carrying two people. The goal of La'Zooz is to encourage drivers to go places not alone but with a passenger, which will help alleviate traffic congestion by taking excess cars off the road. An application of multiple technological paradigms to increase trust and transparency, and do social good.

How about privacy? Many people worry that a huge blockchain database will store personal information about users' travel habits. But the company says that whenever a rider and a driver are matched, only the information that is necessary for their transaction will be available between them. While the network will know everything, users and other people will only be able to access select parts of it.

At the moment, because of its minuscule marketing budget and highly decentralized nature could make it seem unreliable, La'Zooz isn't a threat to established companies such as Uber and Gett, another ride-sharing service in Israel. But as visibility and trust both increase over time, that could change.

As Matan Field, the co-founder of La'Zooz, told *Shareable* blogger Nathan Schneider in January 2015, "Initially we just talked about ridesharing, but from day one we knew that we weren't just speaking about ridesharing. We would try to build a model of participation. Then we stepped into the bitcoin space, and learned about decentralized organizations, and found out that the ideas we were abstractly thinking about had been born and raised on another side of the planet. Ridesharing was just the excuse. There's a whole movement that's going on—a movement for building the future of society, the future of organizations." And then, "With blockchain technology, power is automatically distributed to the whole community. To raise a critical mass of participation, you can invent a token, then distribute that token to whoever contributes. They can be developers, founders, purchasers, or even early adopters. In that way there is an incentive for early participation. Then, as soon as the thing that you are trying to build is operational, there is a critical mass of participants ready to use that same token in the system. In our case, riders will share the cost of a drive with zooz tokens."

Here's what the La'Zooz website says about the effort:

> La'Zooz is a decentralized organization. Anyone can contribute towards the establishment of its goals in whatever way he or she believes would be best. Tasks are carried out within autonomous, self-defined circles or teams. Each circle can consist of any number of individuals (including a single person) collaborating together towards well-defined goals, and holding their own (perhaps multisig) wallet to promote the circle's tasks. Once a circle delivers their contribution, the La'Zooz community as a whole evaluates this contribution and as an expression of appreciation reimburses the circle's wallet with zooz tokens accordingly.

Earlier in this book I talked about the balance between *co-operation* and *control*. Most organizations, from the Catholic Church to Uber, have some proportion of both;

and it's the *control* factor that too often leads to a break-down of trust and even fraud. As we saw in Enron and countless other corporate scandals, too much control in the hands of too few people inevitably fosters secrecy and deception. In contrast, La'Zooz is attempting to operate under something like a modified form of pure democracy. In the literature of La'Zooz we see frequent references to "the community." Active since October 2013, the members of the La'Zooz community have been contributing to the project at different levels and for different time spans. These contributions are ranked by the community, using a reputation system where each member holds a certain "weight." At the end of each month, the members of the La'Zooz community vote on the new weight of each of the other members. The voting process takes place on the La'-Zooz Slack "community votes" channel, through a Google form with the names of all contributors, their scope of work, and their main contacts in the community. At the conclusion of voting, a smart algorithm determines the re-sults of the vote and issues the new weight held by each member of the community.

As of September 2015, about 2,500 people had signed up to use the app. Users have left positive reviews on Twitter and the Google Play, often using such terms as "revolution-ary." Interestingly, the company has reportedly contracted with blue-chip auditors Ernst & Young to provide account-ing services in exchange for digital tokens. The organization currently exists in a sort of limbo between a traditional cor-poration and a true community. As Field told Schneider, until the technology is fully developed, the organization is being run like any other company, with a legal structure that makes it conform to the rules of the protocol. "Of course that's not the ideal solution," said Field, "but it's a middle step before we reach full decentralization." These guys are going to blockchain the crap out of incumbents such as Uber, Lyft, and others just by being a full-fledged decentralized autonomous version of the incumbents!

Music and Art

Israel has emerged as a fertile ground for blockchain-based organizations. As Ahuva Goldstand, Roy Keidar, and Yigal Arnon wrote in "Israel's blockchain startups look to disrupt more than banking" for Venturebeat.com, a Deloitte report released in early 2016 highlighted thirty-eight Israeli start-ups seen to be developing blockchain applications ranging across a wide spectrum of services including social platforms, online commerce, P2P, payments, security, new currency, and hardware. In contrast to many other blockchain startups elsewhere in the world, they've been working closely with large, well-established financial institutions, including big banks. In addition to La'Zooz, the authors focused on the pop music platform Revelator, which tracks music rights and distributes royalties to rights owners in a transparent and reliable way using the blockchain platform from Colu, an emerging digital currency exchange. Revelator gives music creators a way to effectively control their product, rights, and income, effectively removing the middleman—the production and management companies who for generations have locked talent, and especially emerging young artists, into unfair and one-sided contracts. (In fairness, Revelator also pitches itself to those very same producers and managers as a way of keeping better track of their client's assets and royalties. But it can be used by a musician who's a sole proprietor.)

"If you have data every day, why can't we make payments every day?" Revelator founder and CEO Bruno Guez told *Mashable's* Emma Hinchcliffe in September 2016. "If you had a thousand downloads, I can pay you $700 tomorrow."

That speed is made possible by blockchain, said Guez. "The blockchain technology does provide a truly disruptive technology for the music industry. It's not the only thing that matters and it won't solve all the problems in the industry, but I do believe our current offering introduces new features for music."

For visual artists, a San Francisco startup called Blockai is providing an answer to one of the most vexing problems that has plagued the visual arts for centuries: How to assert an owner's copyright protection of a work of art, and on the flip side, how to verify the authenticity of a work of art. In the world of high-priced art sales, the latter is a huge problem. For example, in 2011 one of the oldest and most respected art galleries in America, the Knoedler Gallery in New York, abruptly closed its doors. The reason was the shocking discovery that over the course of fifteen years, the gallery and its president, Ann Freedman, had sold to wealthy collectors forged art worth eighty million dollars. Nearly forty paintings, including seven known as "Spanish elegies" and supposedly created by the artist Robert Motherwell, and which sold for more than $3.5 million, were actually created by forger in his garage in Queens. It was the most audacious and lucrative art fraud in U.S. history—and it could have been prevented with the blockchain protocol.

The following is an excerpt from "80 Million Dollar Con," which aired on May 22, 2016. Anderson Cooper is the correspondent. Greg Clarick is the attorney for a collector who bought a fake Mark Rothko painting for $8 million.

Attorney Greg Clarick: ...The works had no provenance.

Anderson Cooper: No chain, no history?

Greg Clarick: They had no history. They had no documents.

Anderson Cooper: So there was no evidence these paintings had ever been painted by the artists?

Greg Clarick: That's correct.

Clarick went on to say there were no bills of sale, no insurance records, no shipping documents, and no museum exhibitions for any of the paintings. The gallery failed to exercise due diligence—but if Rothko's works had been part of a blockchain record, the buyer could have demanded to see it.

The Blockai offers a very simple process for artists to register their works, ensuring a clear and immutable chain of ownership.

1. You first register your copyright on the blockchain, a public ledger powered by bitcoin. The record is permanent and immutable.

2. You then receive a registration certificate with cryptographic evidence that protects your copyright. You own the certificate forever.

3. You can then sell or distribute your piece of art, with proof of publication that protects your copyright and copyright monitoring that alerts you when a third party uses your work.

The system prevents fraud because if an artist registers all of his or her work, then any work not registered would be known to be a forgery.

Blockchain and Real Estate

You might think that establishing a chain of identity for works of art is a good thing, but let's face it, not everyone is in the market for a Mark Rothko painting with a price tag of $8 million.

But at some point in our lives, just about everyone wants to buy a piece of real estate—a house or a plot of land. And as everyone knows, few things involve more paperwork than buying a piece of real estate.

Ragnar Lifthrasir, president of the International Blockchain Real Estate Association (IBREA), wrote in his 2016 article for *Advisory* entitled "What Is Blockchain and How Does It Apply to Real Estate?" that because of the long list of middlemen, transacting real estate is expensive, opaque, and cumbersome. When buying a piece of property, you have to deal with:

1. Real estate brokers.

2. Government property databases.

3. Title companies: Insurance and property databases.

4. Escrow companies.

5. Inspectors and appraisers.

6. Notary publics.

These are all third-party verifiers of information. They are needed to establish trust and to arrive at a consensus. No trust and no consensus = no deal and no new home for your family.

These middlemen are needed because they hold information that you either can't access or you don't have the necessary permissions required to operate in the existing property transaction space. These records live in separate silos, disconnected from one another until they're printed out on paper, signed, and bundled into a big fat binder that you then place in your safe deposit box, never again to be seen until you or your heirs decide to sell your house.

As Lifthrasir wrote, consider the title to the property. Title information includes the address, previous and current owners, and various encumbrances such as mortgages. These property ownership records are maintained by county recorder offices and title insurance companies. Prior to the Internet, title companies and the government were the only agencies that could record and verify property information.

Blockchain can replace these middlemen by enabling every property, no matter how large or small, to have a unique digital address that contains physical attributes, building performance, legal and financial data, occupancy, and any other pertinent information including the history of repairs to a building. The blockchain conveys this data perpetually and maintains all historical transactions. Additionally, the data can be made available online and can be correlated across all properties.

Consider the title, which is really nothing more than a piece of paper. To transfer a property, you need to fill in the blanks on a deed, sign it with a pen in the presence of a notary who puts his or her seal on it, and then take this paper to the county recorder's office to be placed in their filing cabinet. It's a tedious and time-consuming process that people have been doing since the Middle Ages. Instead of a paper title, the blockchain protocol can create a digital title—a cryptographically secure token that can be transferred as effortlessly, quickly, and cheaply as an email.

We've discussed the ever-present friction of transactions. Imagine the speed to transact a real estate sale being shortened from weeks or months to just a few minutes.

An apt analogy is one of email to snail mail. Prior to email, to write and send a letter you needed a physical chain of products and services. You needed paper and an envelope, a stamp that you bought from the post office, a mailbox to put your letter into, trucks to transport your letter, sorting machines and facilities, and at every stage an army of postal workers to sort and deliver your letter. The cost for a first-class letter is currently forty-nine cents in the Unites States. It's not a terrible deal, but it's a system that's been in place since the United States Postal Service was created on July 26, 1775, by decree of the Second Continental Congress.

The rise of email in the 1990s was the first major advancement in over two hundred years. The digitization and dematerialization of messages disintermediated the snail-mail middlemen and helped close the time and distance gap. The effect on our financial system was huge, as digital money transfers replaced the cumbersome method of mailing checks from one bank to another for verification. But for real estate transactions, the medieval system of paper documents remained untouched. Blockchain can change that. Once buyers and sellers can easily verify property records between each other and transfer a title digitally, then the real estate infrastructure—the armies of brokers, escrow companies, title insurance companies, county recorders, and notary publics—may soon experience the same decline as the post office.

Blockchain creates and intermediary-less marketplace where those who are looking to trust and those who are looking to be trusted can transact with low infrastructure and overhead with very unfamiliar counterparties in very intimate ways.

11. From Consensus to Autonomy

The dictionary defines "autonomy" as "the right or condition of self-government or having its own laws; freedom from external control or influence; independence." Within a blockchain, the infrastructure is no longer controlled by an organization or individual but is broken out over all the points of the network. Therefore, a blockchain is self-supporting and independent from third party services or support. For example, bitcoin relies upon no bank or government to validate it; it simply *is*, and it will exist as long as people use it.

As Geschreven door Ben van Lier wrote in April 2017 in his article for Centric.eu entitled "Blockchain and the Autonomy of Systems," there can be no doubt that "we are readily willing to, in our thinking, swap trusted third parties, as created by humans, for interconnected autonomous technological systems. These interconnected systems can, so we think, jointly make decisions, enter into contracts, and perform information transactions based on their own laws and rules as captured in algorithms for these systems." We're putting increasing levels of trust in the autonomy with which blockchain systems can make decisions based on purpose-built software and algorithms, and, based on such decisions, affect the transfer of value from one participant—individual or organization—to another. But he cautions that when we do so, we must pay attention to the assumptions and preferences that, inevitably, made their way from the human operators into the blockchain. Even a smart contract cannot be "set it and forget it"; there needs to be rigorous quality control at every stage.

Speaking of security and the integrity of things like real estate transactions, in June 2016 WIRED.co.uk published a short article entitled "Blockchain technology will help protect your autonomous car." The article reported on a talk given by Sir Mark Walport, the government chief scientific adviser in the United Kingdom, in which he reminded his audience that vehicle data systems—and especially those of autonomous cars—are highly vulnerable to hacking. Distributed ledgers can prevent self-driving cars from being hacked and having their internal systems exploited. "One thing you don't need is for your autonomous vehicle to be tampered with," he told the WIRED Money conference audience. "In an autonomous car a distributed ledger can be used to protect against compromise of the sensors."

He explained that a centralized system monitored by a distributed ledger would reveal if the systems underpinning an autonomous vehicle, or device that's connected to the internet, have been tampered with. "Distributed ledger technology can help to ensure the security of an asset and ensure it hasn't been tampered with," he said.

New Corporate Models: The Decentralized Autonomous Organization

I've discussed how Uber and other seemingly decentralized corporations can be, in fact, old-fashioned hub-and-spoke aggregators of wealth for the owners. A better choice is emerging; blockchain protocol can, by building trust and then consensus, open the door to new forms of organizations created to pool the energies and talents of people.

A decentralized autonomous organization (DAO), sometimes called a decentralized autonomous corporation (DAC), is an organization that is run through rules encoded as computer programs called smart contracts. A DAO's financial transaction record and program rules are maintained on a blockchain.

The conceptual essence of a decentralized autonomous organization is characterized by the ability of the blockchain protocol to provide an immutable and secure digital ledger that tracks financial interactions across the Internet. It's fortified against forgery or tampering by trusted timestamping and by dissemination of a distributed database. This approach eliminates the need to involve a bilaterally accepted trusted third party in a financial transaction—such as an outside auditor—thus simplifying and streamlining the sequence.

The elimination of both the trusted third party verifier and of the need for repetitive recording of contract exchanges in different records may substantially reduce the costs of a blockchain enabled transaction and of making available the associated data. For example, in principle and if regulatory structures permitted, the blockchain data could replace public documents such as deeds and titles. The blockchain approach allows multiple very unfamiliar parties to enter into loosely coupled peer-to-peer smart contract collaborations in very intimate ways.

How might this work with a ride-sharing company like Uber, where you have countless individual service providers selling their services one at a time to customers?

Instead of a central authority at the hub of the wheel, which is how Uber is organized today, the company—a cooperative, really—would consist of any number of individual operators sharing a blockchain database and set of smart contracts. Let's say a driver who is part of the system is ready to take on a passenger. The driver's client software could propose a cost function, like "find a trusted customer who is within a certain distance of my car." The driver then publishes a smart contract onto the blockchain, which instantly matches ride requests—either pending or new ones coming in—and makes the match. It would be done through a completely open-access industry composed of decentralized ride-sharing cloud computing nodes. The job of the nodes is to use search algorithms to look for ride availabilities and ride requests that score the highest, and submit them. This is not just about reading demand signals early and predicting markets, this is about searching for the demand signals you want, and broadcasting your willingness to supply to customers who didn't know you existed in the first place! Anyone who passes a trust test could participate, with a few nodes providing functions like criminal background checks. The incentive to participate comes from a small fee or bounty paid by the driver through a smart contract to the operator who makes the match and updates the contract in the blockchain.

Once the driver's contract receives the most favorable set of rides and the bounty is paid, the customer's information is passed along to the driver.

As for payment, it could be in traditional currency, like a credit card swiper, or in cryptocurrency like bitcoin or Ethereum. The system, which is managed by its participants, who constantly check on each other and very the accuracy of the blockchain data, produces a high level of trust and eliminates the middleman. No longer would customer payments be taken by the "central office" to then be cycled back to the driver, minus the cut taken by the central office. In today's mobile economy, drivers can take their own payments directly from the passenger. There's no need for the middleman.

Smart Contracts

Since time immemorial, people have been making agreements and contracts with each other. Here's a scene from the Book of Genesis 31:44-45, when Laban says to Jacob: "'So now come, let us make a covenant, you and I, and let it be a witness between you and me.' Then Jacob took a stone and set it up as a pillar." In this pre-literate society, their agreement was marked by a circle of stones with a bigger central stone in the middle. Presumably, it served as a sort of mnemonic device; anyone seeing it would say, "Why the heck is that circle of stones there? Oh yes, now I remember—it was made when Laban and Jacob made their deal."

Ancient Egyptians progressed to written contracts. Here's an excerpt from a contract for the sale of a parcel of farmland executed in 182 BCE. The excerpt is from reshafin.org, edited by André Dolinger. It's a long excerpt, but it's fascinating not only because it exists and gives us a glimpse into ancient lives, but because of the detailed physical descriptions of the parties involved. This was an era before identification cards or Social Security numbers, and the identity of a person could only be verified by examining their physical appearance and clothing, evaluating their answers to questions, and collaborating statements made by trusted individuals. The *agoranomus*, whose name is Paniscus, is the overseer of the *agora*, or market:

> In the 11th which is also the 8th year of the reign of Cleopatra and her son Ptolemy surnamed Alexander, gods Philometores, the priests and priestesses and canephorus being those now in office, on the 28th of the month Paophi, in Crocodilopolis, before Paniscus, agoranomus of the upper toparchy of the Pathyrite nome.
>
> Taous daughter of Harpos, aged about 48 years, of medium height, fair-skinned, round-faced, straight-nosed, with a scar on her forehead, and her sisters Sennesis, also called Tatous daughter of Harpos, aged about 42 years, of medium height, fair-skinned, round-faced, straight-nosed, with a scar on her forehead, and Siephmous daughter of

Pachnoumis, aged about 20 years, fair-skinned, round-faced, straight-nosed, without distinctive mark, all three being Persians, with their guardian, the husband of the aforesaid Taous, Psennesis, also called Krouris son of Florus, Persian of the Epigone, of the village of Gotnit in the lower toparchy of the Latopolite nome, aged about 45 years, of medium height or under, dark-skinned, rather curly-haired, long-faced, straight nosed, with a scar on the under lip, have sold the land, lying inland, corn-bearing, and un-divided, which belongs to them in the north-ern plain of Pathyris and contains three and a half arurae in two plots with the attached surplus out of the 7 in the 40 arurae.

The contract goes on to describe the boundaries of the land in a way that any twenty-first-century land attorney would recognize: "The boundaries of the one plot are, on the south the land of Patous son of Horus and his brothers, on the north the land of Chesthotes son of Melipais, on the east the land of Aes and his brothers, on the west an embank-ment...."

In many ways, the writing and execution of contracts hasn't changed much since Taous and her husband Psennesis sold their land over two thousand years ago. You write down the agreement on papyrus (or paper), sign it, and put it in a filing cabinet or with the appropriate civil authority. Additional actions taken *after* the signing of the contract—

payments, revisions, another sale, a default—need to be created separately. This introduces an element of fallibility. For example, if Psennesis died before the sale was complete, the contract would need to be re-written on a new document. Or if the new landowner later decided to sue Taous and Psennesis and the others because the land was infertile or otherwise unacceptable, that would require an entirely new set of documents not physically linked to the original contract.

Blockchain protocols have the ability to create *smart contracts*. The goal of a smart contract is twofold: to produce a single chained file composed of every iteration of the contract from its inception to the present moment; and to reduce the need for humans to review and act on an agreement over time. In addition, a smart contract can include a software protocol that self-executes an action when consensus on certain conditions are met.

The term "smart contract" was introduced in 1994 by computer scientist Nick Szabo as an attempt to unify what he termed the "highly evolved" practices of contract law and associated business practices with the electronic commerce protocols then emerging between strangers on the Internet.

His original 1994 description is:

"A smart contract is a computerized transaction protocol that executes the terms of a contract. The general objectives are to satisfy common contractual conditions (such as payment terms, liens, confidentiality, and even enforcement), minimize exceptions both malicious and accidental, and minimize the need for trusted intermediaries. Related economic goals include lowering fraud loss, arbitrations and enforcement costs, and other transaction costs."

Contracts become meaningful when value—typically currency or some other asset—is involved. As Vitalik Buterin, the programmer of Ethereum, explained it at the 2016 DC Blockchain Summit, in a smart contract, an asset or currency is legally bound to a program "and the program runs this code, and at some point it automatically validates a condition and it automatically determines whether the asset should go to one person or back to the other person, or whether it should be immediately refunded to the person who sent it or some combination thereof."

Examining a simple real estate transaction can reveal how smart contracts could drastically alter the way business is conducted. Let's say that Lisa and Sam enter into a traditional contract that requires Lisa to pay $300,000 to Sam in exchange for Sam conveying title to his house to Lisa upon receipt of payment. After Lisa pays Sam the money, it's discovered that the house has been flooded many times over the years and the foundation is weak. In fact, it's discovered that Sam had gotten quotes from contractors to fix the hidden water damage, but he hadn't actually made any repairs. Sam refuses to give back the money. Lisa has no choice but to hire an attorney to seek specific performance of the contract, or to obtain damages. A third party, such as a judge, jury, or arbitrator, will make the determination of the outcome. The process is messy and involves countless documents, including the repair bids that Lisa's lawyer must obtain from contractors because Sam hadn't kept them.

Using a smart contract mitigates two possibilities: that vital information is missing (the flooding problem), or that one party will perform (Lisa pays her money) while the other refuses or fails to perform (Sam sells her a defective house). Using a smart contract, Lisa and Sam can agree to the same transaction, but structure it differently. In this scenario, Lisa sees a complete record of the house from the day it was built to the present, including any liens or encumbrances, and even the bids to repair the flood damage. Based on this immutable and complete record and contract, and factoring in the cost of foundation repairs, Lisa agrees to pay $250,000 worth of virtual currency to Sam, who agrees to transmit the title to the house. When Lisa transfers the virtual currency to Sam, this action serves as the triggering event for the smart contract, which then automatically sends the title to the house to Lisa. The transfer is then complete, and Lisa's ownership of the house is verifiable through a publically available record on the blockchain.

Structuring this transaction as a smart contract on the blockchain ensures that there are no missing or hidden documents, the transfer of title occurs as soon as funds are received, and the publically available, verifiable record of the transfer is automatically updated. Because the contract automatically executes according to the rules agreed to by Lisa and Sam, there is little risk of deception, and no requirement for third-party verification of the underlying facts because there's nothing hidden or vague, and the contract, which is not just a dated agreement but a complete history of the house and its ownership, is available as a public document.

Trust, consensus and autonomous commerce can create new opportunities for exciting organizations to operate differently, and this is both promising and exiting. What truly energizes me is the notion that blockchain will enable new types templates of how we organize and govern to cooperate as a species. Instead of just being to select form a dozen archetypes of corporate structures such as S-Corps, C-Corps or Limited Liability Corporation, I expect that we will start to design, mature and recognize a few dozen thousand types of new corporate archetypes.

New archetypes of corporations that are born trusted, only operating transparently, and can compete in new marketplace structures built on reconfigured digitized and dematerialized remnants left from the massacred of today's existing companies and industries.

12. The Future: Trust Companies

If you ask Marc Benioff what is at the core of Salesforce, the chairman and CEO of the company he founded, you may assume his answer might be something about being a cloud company or a customer relationship (CRM) company. After all, the cloud is the logo of Salesforce. I'm sure that Marc will say Salesforce is a *customer company*. There is an effect that swept through commerce globally after the arrival of Salesforce. Every company in the world started to focus on being more customer-centric.

A customer company is simply one that proactively engages its customers across the same platforms that they use every day. Aside from listening to your customers and providing them with a positive and consistent experience, you must be able to have an ongoing relationship with your customers across every channel. With today's world so keen on social connectivity, engaging your customers socially is increasingly important.

Much like Salesforce led the charge for all of commerce to become customer companies, someone will lead the charge for all of commerce to become *trust companies*.

While the cloud, mobility, social media, and big data enabled the ability for customer companies to emerge, blockchain will enable trust companies to emerge.

What's a trust company?

At the core of a trust company are three things:

1. An aggregation of datum that is transparent.

2. Consensus that is easy.

3. Autonomy that can scale.

Thus far in the book we've discussed the impact of financial and accounting data being stored on a blockchain, and the unprecedented impact this could have on commerce and human cooperation. As additional sets of data such as identity data, reputation data, inventory data, market data, agreement data, cooperate data, and others evolve through the blockchain maturity model of trust, consensus, and autonomy, commerce and human cooperation will change even more fundamentally.

Blockchain Institutional Revolution Maturity Model

	Finance Data	Identity Data	Reputation Data	Inventory Data	Market Data	Agreement Data	Cooperate Data
TRUST	1A						
CONSENSUS							
AUTONOMY							7C

As we move from left to right in the maturity model represented in the table above, we would experience increasingly disruptive new business models, and in addition as we move from top to bottom in the maturity model represented in the table above we would experience exponentially disruptive new market structures. At the time of this writing, I estimate we are currently on the top left (cell 1A) of the table above; this is where most of the focus is from IBM Hyperledger, Ethereum, R3 Corda, Sawthooth, Ripple, and others. The massacre happens as we approach the bottom right (cell 7C) of the table above.

Here are details of the data sets that will be put on blockchains moving left to right in the table above and then progressing top to bottom in the table above evolving those data sets through being trusted, enjoying easy consensus, and eventually being candidates for smart contracts to act on autonomously.

Finance

We've discussed how the old method of proprietary journal keeping invites secrecy and even fraud. Within the designated stakeholder circle (it's understood that some corporate finances, such as research & development programs, need to be obscured from public view), blockchain ledgers for recording and storing financial information are more accessible and less easy to falsify. It's hard to imagine how the Enron scandal could have been pulled off if the company's accounts had been on blockchain ledgers. Likewise for Worldcom, the US telecom company that collapsed in 2002 in one of the largest accounting frauds in history. The company kept two sets of accounts—one to impress Wall Street investors and another secret set that recorded the ugly reality. As the Federal Bankruptcy Court wrote, "As enormous as the fraud was, it was accomplished in a relatively mundane way: more than $9 billion in false or unsupported accounting entries were made in WorldCom's financial systems in order to achieve desired reported financial results." Such a fraud is made possible when a company's account ledgers exist in a universe unto themselves, disconnected from reality. It's precisely this type of fraud that the use of a blockchain protocol can prevent.

Identity

According to the Worldbank, in developing nations there are 2.4 billion low-income people, of which 1.5 billion are adults or are over the age of fourteen, who don't have a form of verifiable personal identification. While *they* know who they are, they can't *prove* it, which means that they're often shut out from owning property, moving across borders, and accessing social safety nets. They're more vulnerable to crime and corruption, including human trafficking and even slavery. In developing nations, because there are few proven holders of property rights, without a system of proper personal identification a modern market economy is impossible to create.

Blockchain technology can be applied to identity applications in areas including online account logins, personal IDs, wedding and birth certificates, e-residency, and passports. By combining the decentralized blockchain architecture with identity verification, a digital ID can be created to act as a digital signature, which can be assigned to every online transaction of any asset.

Does this idea seem farfetched? Not to the people of Estonia. Since its independence from the Soviet Union in 1991, this nation of 1.3 million souls has become something of a highly advanced digital state. Citizens of Estonia are provided with free education, universal health care, and the longest paid maternity leave in the OECD. The country has developed a robust IT sector, and is one of the world's most digitally advanced societies. In 2005 Estonia became the first nation to hold elections over the Internet, and in 2014 the first to provide e-residency, which allows non-Estonians access to Estonian services including banking, company formation, taxation, and payment processing.

In 2007, the tiny Baltic state introduced secure, authenticated identity as the birthright of every Estonian. At the moment of birth, the hospital issues a digital birth certificate and the baby's health insurance starts automatically. All residents aged fifteen and older have electronic ID cards, which are used in electronic banking, signing contracts, health care access, shopping, encrypting email, as railway tickets, and even to vote.

As just one example, you'll remember my story about coming to America to enroll in college, being told I was missing two vaccinations on my medical report, and then simply temporarily writing them in myself? This couldn't happen in Estonia, where the government has launched DreamApply, a blockchain-based student recruitment and marketing system which seeks to streamline the application and admissions process for college students. A system like

DreamApply would have flagged the fact that I was missing two vaccinations *at the moment I applied*—which would be a lot better than finding out when I showed up to register for classes.

Can Estonia's program be scaled up? The European Union is moving in Estonia's direction. As *The Economist* reported in June 2014, "What may provide the necessary scale is a European Union rule soon to come into force that will require member states to accept each others' digital IDs. That means non-resident holders of Estonian IDs, wherever they are, will be able not only to send each other encrypted email and to prove their identity to web service providers who accept government-issued identities, but also to do business with governments anywhere in the EU."

Big corporations are taking note as well. Nasdaq announced in January 2017 that following the example of an election pilot project in Estonia, blockchain technology can safely be used to authenticate e-voting by shareholders at a company's annual general meeting.

As Shaun Waterman reported in *Cyberscoop*, "the stock market technology provider—which has a subsidiary that runs a securities market and ownership registry in Estonia's capital, Tallinn—said in a report it had successfully built and operated four web-based user interfaces that allowed shareholders in Estonia to log in using their verified national online ID and vote at the AGM of Tallinn-listed tech company LVH Group."

Estonia's sophisticated e-ID program, which provides its citizens with an electronic token to enable secure identity verification online, was seen as critical to the pilot's success. The Estonia pilot used blockchain technology to record the ownership of securities as reported by the Estonian central securities depository, or (CSD), the ownership registry operated by Nasdaq Tallinn.

Reputation

Identity is important, and reputation equally so. After all, the plumber who comes to your house may very well be exactly who he says he is—but how about his reputation? Is he trustworthy, or a con artist?

Reputation can be compared to a trust score. A blockchain-based reputation system can provide a range of data points that can be used by different applications to determine an appropriate reputation for the given task. For example, if you're a La'Zooz customer looking for a driver at midnight, being able to verify the driver has a perfect driving record and no criminal history would be very reassuring.

If you're a bank, and you're required to follow the know-your-customer (KYC) protocol, confirming the customer's identity is mandatory, but how about reputation? Things like credit history, bankruptcies, and criminal convictions will impact how you do business with that person. Today, to compile a reputation profile of a person you need to go to multiple sources—credit reporting agencies, the police department, the courts, schools, state motor vehicle department, previous employers, all of which have information stored in separate silos. A blockchain reputation management program could bring all of those together.

How about those review sites that offer everything from high praise to vicious attacks, and all anonymously? Fake reviews have become ubiquitous. Yelp has been actively questioned for how it handles fake reviews, and on Amazon fake reviews had become so pervasive that the company now aggressively fights them. Bazaarvoice, the network that connects brands and retailers to (as the website says) "the authentic voices of people where they shop," has a team dedicated to eradicating them.

By applying distributed ledger technology, reviews can deliver trustworthy endorsements. For example, The World Table, a Utah-based startup that specializes in online reputation services, has launched Open Reputation, a quantified reputation system to aggregate reputation data and report trust scores for individuals and organizations. A decentralized platform, it's supported by an online community and an open-source project.

As John Carosella, CMO at The World Table, explained in May 2015 on InsideBitcoins, "The Open Reputation architecture mandates that identities and reputes (reputation events—things like ratings) are indexed (and in some cases stored) using blockchain technologies so they're not forgeable and not 'owned' by any single player." This builds greater autonomy, trust, and freedom.

Inventory

Earlier in this book I offered my story about tangerines, and how nice it would be if the tangerine I bought in the store had a QR code stuck on it that would tell me the little guy's complete history—where it was grown, if any pesticides were used, and how it was shipped.

This is a form of supply chain control that blockchain makes possible. From smart contracts that make payments and trigger audits to the tracking of inventory and assets, the blockchain protocol promises to enable greater supply chain efficiency. Every time an object moves through the supply chain, the transaction would be documented, creating a permanent history of that product from manufacture (or, in the case of the tangerine, planting and harvesting) to sale. This could dramatically cut delays, lower costs, and reduce the human error that plague transactions today. Documenting a product's migration through the supply chain preserves a record of its true origin and touchpoints, increasing trust and helping to eliminate the ambiguity found in today's fragmentary supply chains.

A Mountain View, California company called Skuchain is offering what it calls "cryptographically secure smart contracts governing all phases of trade agreements," described by their acronym BRACKETS, or "Blockchain-based Release of funds that Are Conditionally Key-signed, and Triggered by Signals." The solution impacts not only the creation and preservation of records, such as with my tangerine, but also reduces friction all along the supply chain. Friction that slows a supply chain can come from many sources: inspections, payments, releases, verifications, or mistakes. Their BRACKETS system and its smart contracts can bring increased transparency for all participants while providing a real-time, reliable view of each stage of a transaction, helping stakeholders build a more trustworthy and stable supply chain ecosystem.

Market

Big data. It's the term that, to many people, has become synonymous with Godzilla. It's an uncontrollable monster, ready to devour every inch of database storage with content that's 1% useful and 99% garbage.

More soberly, it's both a technical and marketing term that refers to a valuable organizational asset—the distillation of actionable information from masses of data. It represents a trend in technology that is spearheading a new approach in making business decisions and understanding the world.

Business decisions are increasingly being made after the analysis of very large amounts of both structured and unstructured data including non-spreadsheet data like videos, tweets, and commercial transactions, which have become difficult to process using traditional database and information management tools.

But all too often, big data can lead to big confusion, because of the difficulty in transforming mountains of data to actionable information. As *Computer Weekly* noted in 2013, "Big data has not yet led to big outcomes. Despite all the hype, less than half of all employees find that corporate information helps them get their jobs done. The problem of getting the right information to the right people at the right time is getting worse with the growing number of information sources, uses, and users."

Take just one example—the public utilities, and in particular electric power companies. Their universe of data has recently been compounded by the emergence of millions of individual homes—electricity consumers—that are now also electricity *providers*. Suddenly the grid is a two-way street, with energy flowing both to and from customers. Companies can't possibly manage this data by having a guy come to your house twice a year to read your meter. A method that's much more powerful is needed.

As James Basden and Michael Cottrell wrote in March 2017 for *The Harvard Business Review*, blockchain technology has become instrumental in managing this tsunami of data. "In New York state," they wrote, "neighbors are testing their ability to sell solar energy to one another using blockchain technology. In Austria, the country's largest utility conglomerate, Wien Energie, is taking part in a blockchain trial focused on energy trading with two other utilities. Meanwhile in Germany, the power company Innogy is running a pilot to see if blockchain technology can authenticate and manage the billing process for autonomous electric-vehicle charging stations." These are new corporate archetypes, and new market structures that are emerging as we digitize and dematerialize today's industries. If the new digitized and dematerialized assets can be trusted, both early supply and demand signals will create massive competitive white spaces in in reconstructed trusted commerce.

Even in such complex situations—or perhaps *especially* in such complex situations—blockchain could offer a dependable and trustworthy way for operational and financial transactions to be recorded in real time and validated across a distributed network with no central point of authority. As in the financial services industry, it may be possible that blockchain can simplify the business of utilities by eliminating the need for intermediaries altogether. As the authors write, "blockchain technology may ultimately accelerate the transition to what the energy industry calls a 'distributed world' made up of both large and smaller power-generation systems for homes, businesses, and communities."

Agreement

Every company incorporated in the United States has an underlying set of bylaws. These are the rules by which corporations organize and are governed. For example, a company's bylaws can dictate when shareholder meetings are communicated and how those meetings are conducted. Bylaws can include the rules of reporting the health and performance information of a company, who can vote on what decisions, and what roles and hierarchical structures must exist in an organization for it to operate transparently.

Bylaws are put in place to ensure that organizations operate responsibly, and standards are met that protect investors, consumers, and the public from corporations amassing and then misusing menacing amounts of power. Today, most of these bylaws are loosely interpreted, and employees, consumers, shareholders, and the public are rarely aware of how well or not a corporation abides by them.

Imagine a world where corporate information was trusted and transparent. In an era of Enron and Bernie Madoff, is such a thing difficult to visualize? Think about corporate bylaws, and how they are written and then rarely looked at. They're regarded as more of an annoyance, or a ceremonial step on the way to ringing the opening bell at the New York Stock Exchange. Too often today, bylaws are printed documents that are created only so that companies can get legally incorporated, and then no one reads them.

Imagine if corporate bylaws were loaded up on a blockchain, where all the company's investors, employees, and customers could read them and see how they are used to organize and govern. It would be like looking into the moral rule set of a corporation.

Why isn't this done today, and what could it look like if it were done?

How we organize has been driven by consensus derived from trusted data. Some companies organize in flat structures, and techniques like "span of control" are used to inform how we organize. Why do we need such complex organizational structures and charts? Instead of structure informing strategy, perhaps strategy should inform structure. We can ask, what would organizational structure look like if it were easy to arrive at high quality decisions driven by consensus?

We can guess that the org structure or chart would look less like a pyramid and more like a constellation.

How we govern would be more autonomous, with an improvement over the slow pace of decision making, the slow rate of change, and the amount of deception in those that influence decisions. To help accelerate business processes, decisions can be made when data is easily available on the facts and evidence, removing the need for ideas to be "sold" to leadership before they are voted on.

Many more data sets will emerge on blockchains. IBM CEO Ginni Rometty has put a blockchain in place internally to track the company's $40 billion in financing. The technology is being used to manage disputes and build trust—as she said, it's for "anywhere you're trading some set of assets and need to be sure about the authenticity."

At the FinTech Ideas Festival, Microsoft CEO Satya Nadella shed light on some of the ways in which blockchain is impacting the digital industry. Microsoft is in the process of strengthening the company's blockchain strategy, including the blockchain marketplace ecosystem.

And as *Blockchain Technology News* reported in March 2017, Microsoft, Intel, British Petroleum, J.P. Morgan, Wipro, and Accenture are among the companies that have formed the Enterprise Ethereum Alliance, a group dedicated to the advancement of the blockchain protocol and connecting startups, academics, technology vendors, and Fortune 500 enterprises with Ethereum subject matter experts.

To get a high definition grasp on the full impact of the Institutional Revolution being driven by blockchain, let's look at how corporate data would traverse through trust, consensus, and autonomy.

Cooperate

As we have discussed, humans have long balanced the need for cooperation with the need for corporate control in a hierarchy of power. Most corporate hierarchies call for directors and officers who may or may not be sufficient to follow the bylaws and govern the allocation of resources to coordinate, create, and capture value. Most corporations organize a team of leaders and managers that goes far beyond the officers and directors called for in corporate bylaws. Layers of chief executive officers, presidents, executive vice presidents, executive directors, and vice presidents of everything are organized in order to follow the corporate bylaws and manage resources and value creation.

Sometimes external management consultants are hired, and in some companies spending on leadership and management is two or three times more than what is spent on those who do the work. This is where the "organization chart" comes into play. If you are anything like me, you have been employed at the bottom, middle, and top of the organization chart. And at each level of the organization chart, you might have asked yourself how is it that no one else can see how wasteful this formation is, or how this formation actually impedes the creation of value instead of driving it.

The issue is, the data that represents how we organize is not easily transparent, decisions of how we organize are not made with consensus, and the ability to change the structure of how we organize can take months, if not years.

Changing the organization chart autonomously at scale? Woah, what? How would that even work?

The governance of an organization is the final safeguard against a sub-optimal organization chart. Governance is more about decision-making and the wielding of power and influence and less about reporting structure. Somewhere between the organization chart and the governance model of a corporation is the true center of gravity of its culture and propensity to stick to its stated strategy, and its execution of its mission to bring a vision to life.

Governance is powered by decision-making, and influence relies on data. Data about the cost of a project, the return on investments of a business case, the performance of a person, department, business unit or division, and risk and alternatives are all inputs into good governance.

Take, for example, one of the more viable decisions that must be governed in an organization: the size, shape, and complexion of the annual budget. Are those who make the decisions on budgets the best suited to make them? Are the business cases put forth truthful enough to drive decisions, or have the underlying data for business cases been tampered with in PowerPoint? I personally have adopted the habit of starting in the back section of PowerPoint presentations that are brought forward to me. This is because I suspect this is where all of the really hairy information is hidden in a PowerPoint presentation. The front section is usually where all of the massaging of the data is done, to make the story sound better than it actually is.

If the example on annual budgets is not enough to show the gaps in how we govern today, think about the annual employee performance review process in organizations, and the force ranking on a bell curve across departments and departments, divisions, and business units.

I know what you're thinking—please, let's not go there!

The Future: Trust Companies

Much like the customer company lead by Marc Benioff from Salesforce.com was unimaginable just fifty years ago, for some people trust companies may be unimaginable today.

In 1967—fifty years ago of this writing—the notion of social listening, a 360-degree multi-channel and multi-stakeholder view of a customer, targeting, and segmentation of real time offers, and social or wisdom of crowd buying were all difficult customer company capabilities to imagine. In 1967, things were very different than they are today. Major news stories included world's first heart transplant, the first ATM, strikes by American teachers for pay increases, the first Super Bowl played between Green Bay Packers and the Kansas City Chiefs, The Six-Day War when Arab forces attacked Israel, and beginning the Yom Kippur War; and the average price of a movie ticket in the US was $1.25.

In fifty years, much has happened to commerce. Most of it has taken the form of an Information Revolution that included cloud, mobile, social, big data, and some form of AI, enabling emergent customer companies.

Let us think fifty years ahead to 2067, and imagine what a trust company may look like in the Institutional Revolution.

1. What is the new role of a CEO in a trust company? Will there be one?

2. What is the role of human resources in a trust company? Will LinkedIn still be needed?

3. What is the role of an auditor in a trust company? Will Ernst & Young still be in business?

The time is coming when every business owner will need to ask themselves, "What would my company look like in a world where the blockchain protocol were commonplace?" Blockchain is poised to transform the traditional business structure whereby work is done via command and control. Instead of a pyramid with the CEO at the top and layers of management below, the blockchain-based organization would be comprised of a seamless network of coordinated freelancers. Instead of a hierarchy of bosses, collaborators will be able to work together as free agents.

Today's companies grow until they get so large that the cost of doing a transaction *inside* the company—the pyramid— becomes higher than that of doing it on a collaborative basis—the constellation.

The Internet reduced much of the friction of time and space, allowing companies to grow larger, both internally and by adding external remote and freelance workers. But the traditional control function remained, with the ubiquitous pyramid form of the CEO supported by expanding layers of management. The Internet did not solve the problem of the people at the top of the pyramid being secretive or even engaging in fraud.

Blockchain makes it possible for the pyramid to flatten out and assume a new shape—the constellation. Blockchain eases the need for supervisory control by creating a transparent record of reality: who performed what task for whom, or who paid how much and when. With each action, it instantly updates its internal picture of the state of the world.

Our existing business processes and governance structures were designed in an age when the pyramid form was the most efficient and productive. But times have changed. Blockchain has the potential to redefine every function within an organization and, over time, transform the structure of the corporation. There will be less energy required for control, and therefore more energy available for productivity.

It is not just the structure of the organization or the archetype of the institution that blockchain changes; it is the efficiency of the marketplace that will create new whitespace opportunities to compete and disrupt.

In 1937 economist Ronald Coase proposed in his article for *Economica* entitled "The Nature of the Firm" that corporations exist because markets can't do everything efficiently; many tasks are easier and cheaper to do within a corporation. When you need repeatable work done, it can be more cost effective to hire and train staff in a corporation rather than contract with freelancers.

However, Coase warned that there would be "decreasing returns to the entrepreneur function," including increasing overhead costs and increasing friction in transactions which will stand as hurdles on the road to efficient markets. Coase argued that the cost of transactions inhibits market efficiencies, and as a result suggested that the lowering of transaction costs (if possible) will render unimaginable market self-selection for efficiency.

Perhaps, what Coase did not consider is the improvement to market efficiencies from increased trust in transactions.

Coase brilliantly articulated that lower transaction costs would more likely lead to markets that would self-select to a state of Pareto efficiency. We have seen a significant lowering of transaction costs largely fueled by the Internet, but our markets are not as close to Pareto efficiencies as Coase imagined in 1937. At the time of his writing, it would have been nearly impossible for Coase to recognize that at some point trust would eventually be abundant in transactions because of blockchain. And, that markets would more likely self-select into Pareto efficiencies as a result of highly trusted transactions; and not necessarily as a result of just lowering transaction costs. This new trusted state of commerce will enable new institution archetypes and corporate structures to transact at low cost and high speed with *unfamiliar counterparties in a trusted and intimate manner*. Such trusted and frictionless markets would render virtually every asset, value, right, or privilege as a liquid good exchangeable form some return value.

It's like the leap we took from sailing ships to steamships. Just like the crew of a square-rigger spent much of their energy handling the sails, a traditional company expended much of its human energy in managing its operations. In the coming Institutional Revolution, blockchain companies will be more productive, require less managerial control, and foster a greater level of trust from customers, employees, and counterparties.

This is the Institutional Revolution.

Every company is at risk of being disrupted by a trusted version of itself.

CPSIA information can be obtained
at www.ICGtesting.com
Printed in the USA
BVOW06*1926090118
504350BV00013B/85/P